Ways In
Approaches to Reading and Writing about Literature

Ways In

Approaches to Reading and Writing about Literature

Gilbert H. Muller

The City University of New York
LaGuardia

John A. Williams

Rutgers University

McGraw-Hill, Inc.

New York   St. Louis   San Francisco   Auckland   Bogotá
Caracas   Lisbon   London   Madrid   Mexico City   Milan
Montreal   New Delhi   San Juan
Singapore   Sydney   Tokyo   Toronto

This book was developed by STEVEN PENSINGER, Inc.

Ways In
Approaches to Reading and Writing about Literature

Permissions Acknowledgments appear on pages 105–106, and on this page by reference.

This book is printed on acid-free paper.

5 6 7 8 9 0   DOC   DOC   9 0 9 8 7 6

ISBN 0-07-044203-7

This book was set in Times Roman by Ruttle, Shaw & Wetherill, Inc.
The editors were Steve Pensinger and James R. Belser;
the production supervisor was Diane Ficarra.
The cover was designed by Karen K. Quigley.
R. R. Donnelley & Sons Company was printer and binder.

Cover credit: ''Interior with Housemaid'' by Vanessa Bell, 1939. Copyright Williamson Art
     Gallery and Museum, Birkenhead, Merseyside.

Library of Congress Cataloging-in-Publication Data

Muller, Gilbert H., (date).
   Ways in: approaches to reading and writing about literature /
Gilbert H. Muller, John A. Williams.
      p.   cm.
   Includes index.
   ISBN 0-07-044203-7
   1. English language—Rhetoric.   2. Literature—History and
criticism—Theory, etc.   3. Criticism—Authorship.   I. Williams,
John A. (John Alfred), (date).   II. Title.
PE1479.C7M85   1994
808'.0668–dc20   93-1666

About the Authors

Gilbert H. Muller, who received a Ph.D. in English and American Literature from Stanford University, is currently professor of English and special assistant to the president at the LaGuardia campus of the City University of New York. He has also taught at Stanford, Vassar, and several universities overseas. Dr. Muller is the author of the award-winning *Nightmares and Visions: Flannery O'Connor and the Catholic Grotesque, Chester Himes,* and other critical studies. His essays and reviews have appeared in *The New York Times, The New Republic, The Nation, The Sewanee Review, The Georgia Review,* and elsewhere. He is also a noted author and editor of textbooks in English and composition, including *The Short Prose Reader* with Harvey Wiener and, with John A. Williams, *The McGraw-Hill Introduction to Literature* and *Bridges: Literature across Cultures.* Among Dr. Muller's awards are National Endowment for the Humanities Fellowships, a Fulbright Fellowship, and a Mellon Fellowship.

John A. Williams, the Paul Robeson Professor of English at Rutgers University, is the author of twelve novels, among them *The Man Who Cried I Am* (1967), *¡Click Song* (1982), *Jacob's Ladder* (1987), and *Trio: Clifford's Blues* (1994), as well as ten nonfiction works that include studies on Richard Wright and Martin Luther King, Jr. (1970), Richard Pryor (1991), and Malcolm X (1993). In addition, he has edited or coedited ten books, among them *The McGraw-Hill Introduction to Literature* (1985). A former journalist, Williams is also a poet and playwright and a recipient of the Rutgers University Lindback Foundation Award for Distinguished Teaching.

To
Laleh, Parisa, and Darius
and to
Lori, Greg, Dennis, and Adam
and as well to
Margo, John Gregory, Nancy, and David

Contents

Preface

Writing and reading are not all that distinct for a writer. Both exercises require being alert and reading for unaccountable beauty, for the intricateness or simple elegance of the writer's imagination, for the world that the imagination evokes.

Toni Morrison
Playing in the Dark

Ways In introduces students to the nature of literary and cultural inquiry. It highlights in an accessible way the recursive nature of the reading and writing processes, while enhancing awareness of the relationship between a writer's personal voice and his or her culture. As a text bridging the gap between literary and composition theory, *Ways In* is a concise, integrated guide to critical reading, thinking, and writing about literature.

In this text we focus on the processes whereby students can explore the diversity of voices that they encounter in our companion anthologies, *Bridges: Literature across Cultures* and *The McGraw-Hill Introduction to Literature.* Many of the literary examples presented in *Ways In*, ranging from Sophocles' *Oedipus Rex* to the provocative sketch "Girl" by Jamaica Kincaid, reflect the multicultural ethos governing our interconnected texts. By stressing the many cultural contexts for composition, we root the reading and writing processes in considerations of race, gender, class, ethnicity, and region.

Because of this multicultural emphasis, *Ways In* can be a useful ancillary text for any literature course. Moreover, by engaging students in the actual stages of the reading and writing processes, while considering the basic elements of fiction, poetry, and drama, we offer a comprehensive guide tailored to the needs and expectations of today's diverse student population. Strategies for making discoveries about literature (and discoveries about oneself) are given priority, from reading critically and responding to literature to planning, drafting, and revising compositions.

Throughout *Ways In,* students are encouraged to think about literature and then apply those discourse strategies appropriate to the critical tasks at hand. The text teaches students how to develop critical approaches to literature—whether feminist, historicist, psychological, reader-response, or any other—and how to apply this knowledge, as well as an understanding of the elements of fiction, poetry, and drama to their writing. We offer detailed guidance on the stages of the writing process, as well as explanations of personal, informative, analytical, and argumentative strategies for critical discourse. Examples of student and professional writing provide detailed guidance. From discussions of precis and summary writing to the writing of critical research papers, we attempt constantly to connect critical thinking and problem-solving skills to different writing situations.

The materials and methods of *Ways In* provide students with a text that they can relate to and that builds their confidence as writers in literature and combined literature-and-composition courses. The text emphasizes the reader's involvement with literature and authentic responses to fiction, poetry, and drama. It teaches students to deal wisely and well with the diversity of their literary culture.

Gilbert H. Muller
John A. Williams

PART ONE

Critical Reading and Writing

1

Reading and Responding to Literature

How about writing a composition for me, for English? I'll be up the creek if I don't get the goddam thing in by Monday.

from *The Catcher in the Rye* by J.D. Salinger

Thus does Holden Caulfield's schoolmate, Stradlater, lament the need to submit a composition for his English class. You may view writing essays for English in a similar fashion. On the other hand, you may see the task as a challenge: you must generate your own thoughts and opinions; harness, arrange, and organize them; and transform them into effective writing. The end product in this writing process should be an essay that clearly expresses your views, insights, discoveries, and reflections. Regardless of your view of the issue, this text is designed to provide you with an understanding of the processes involved in writing about literature. You will learn strategies for applying these processes to your own writing; hopefully, you will gain a greater appreciation for critical writing about literature (even if your opinions about English composition initially resemble those of Stradlater's).

WHAT IS LITERATURE?

First of all, what has come to be known as *literature* is writing in prose or verse that contains complex yet coherent ideas and meanings; deals with universal issues that are significant to an audience; is written in an original and imaginative way; and is of interest to a large number of educated readers. Who decides if a work—whether fiction, poetry, drama, or essay—meets these criteria? Basically, experts decide the quality of any endeavor. These individuals have spent much time studying, analyzing, discussing, and applying the specialized vocabulary of criticism to literature.

Of course, there is also a subjective component in literary criticism. Literary judgments are based on personal taste even though such tastes have been molded by conventional standards. This is a bit different from being an expert in a less subjective field like sports. A sprinter who can run the 100-meter dash in 10.0 seconds is obviously top-notch while another who runs the same distance in 12.0 seconds would not be considered a world-class competitor. With literature, it is more difficult to be certain of your opinions about what is good or mediocre. However, if a work stands the test of time like Sophocles' *Oedipus Rex* or *Othello* by Shakespeare, you may assume that generations of readers have returned to these works and found them personally meaningful and of literary merit. This quality of literature to endure is what the writer Ezra Pound was referring to when he stated that "Literature is news that stays news."

Today, however, there is much debate over the idea of the *canon*, that is, the body of work we believe to be deemed literature. Many argue that what is considered literature is merely the narrow-minded view of a group of like-minded individuals from a more-or-less similar social class, with homogeneous values, who share a similar outlook on life and art. In other words, why have certain literary works been accepted, read and taught over centuries, while others have either vanished or have been ignored? This argument embraces cultures, genres, and social classes. Nonetheless, newly discovered or rediscovered works often make for exciting and provocative reading; only the future will tell us whether they will enter the body of writing we call literature. Take for example the work of Kate Chopin. Her short stories, for example "A Respectable Woman" in your anthology, and novels like *The Awakening* were neglected for many years; however, a couple of decades ago, critics began to view her work as explorations of feminism that were ahead of their time, so that now her fiction is read and discussed widely. Or consider the case of Emily Dickinson. Virtually unknown while she was alive, today she is considered to be one of America's greatest poets.

READING AND THINKING CRITICALLY

To write intelligently about literature, you must first read actively and think critically about it. But why does literature require such reading and reflection? Good literature forces you to enter into a dialogue with it. The themes, style, content, meanings, and structure of true literature challenge you intellectually and imaginatively. Other forms of writing usually do not.

You *can* read a story or novel straight through for entertainment, sensing that you have easily extracted all its meaning, derived from it all its pleasure. This is popular literature—crime fiction, romance novels, westerns, science fiction—and you *consume* these forms. When you are done, you find yourself satisfied for the time being. You put the book down, often not to pick it up again. Conversely, with truly significant literature, you not only read it, but also think about it, ask questions about it. How do you know if what you are reading requires such an effort? If you find yourself thinking about what you have read; if you feel the need to review some or all of it for deeper comprehension; if there are elements such as character, theme, plot, style, and other literary components that have you curious or perplexed, the work is more likely to be literary.

Informed readers of literature usually automatically ask themselves certain basic, key questions about what they are reading. The following questions can help you grasp the significant elements of what you are reading and serve as springboards to pursue further and more detailed issues in the text.

1. What is the author's purpose?

A Raisin in the Sun has been viewed as one of the first plays that simultaneously brought the plight and strength of the African-American family to light for mainstream America. Was that the purpose of Lorraine Hansberry, the playwright? Was the play's purpose to evoke sympathy, outrage, or was it meant to engage its audience in an evening of riveting theater, one that would make them raise issues about their own attitudes toward racism? Or possibly did the playwright have in mind breaking racial stereotypes that many white Americans had about African-American families? All these would be worthy purposes. But without the author directly stating his or her purpose, we must infer it. The value of inquiring about purpose is that it can assist you in understanding the *theme* of what you read.

2. What is the author's theme or main idea?

The theme of Raymond Carver's short story "Cathedral" is that an individual whose perception is limited psychologically can be blind to reality while a truly blind person may have a rich experience of reality. If that statement seems emphatic, it was meant to be. It is one person's summing up of his interpretation of a work of fiction. The term "theme" is sometimes referred to as an author's main idea or major statement or "what the author is trying to say." Regardless of what term you use, you should be cautious in assuming that the theme *you* have determined to be the correct one is the only valid one. Of course, common sense and rational thought will prevent one from accepting *any* theme as possible; still, there may be more than one acceptable one. Stating your interpretation of a theme of a work of literature and then writing about it is an important step toward understanding what you read. It is often the starting and end point for making sense of a work of literature. Discovering a theme gives your reading clarity so that all the elements of what you read are more easily and succinctly comprehended.

3. What is the emotional effect of the writing?

Critics and philosophers have been concerned with the emotional effect of literature since the Greek philosopher Aristotle discussed the issue in his *Poetics* some 2500 years ago. He referred to the concept of *catharsis* as that emotion one experiences when watching a drama that purges one of pent-up emotions. Identification, anger, glee, sadness are all emotions that may be evoked by literature. In fact, tragedy and comedy, two modes of dramatic literature, are often defined by them. Your emotional response to literature will most probably be tempered by your own personality and life experience, perhaps even your gender. For years, critics called Hemingway a "man's writer" because his work portrayed stoic men who endured life without complaint. His story, "A Clean, Well-Lighted Place" in your anthology, is a fine example of this. Do you identify with the older waiter? If so, how much has it to do with whether you are a man or woman? How much does it have to do with whether you yourself feel lonely or not and how you regard your loneliness? Raising questions about the emotional effect of writing helps you understand what you read and can assist you in understanding yourself as well.

4. What biases or ideological viewpoints do you detect?

Many students of literature claim that *all* authors have a personal bias and/ or an ideological viewpoint that bears on their writing. For example, the mere fact that a writer has had a college education places him or her in a certain class, and therefore places that writer in a particular educational class. For your purposes, it is probably better to consider the bias or ideological leanings of a writer based on his or her gender; economic class; racial and ethnic background, and political viewpoint. Some authors present such viewpoints in more obvious ways than others. For example, Langston Hughes, an African American, was often critical of American society; if you read his play *Soul Gone Home* you will discover a humorous, lucid, and straightforward critique of class and caste. On the other hand, the short story "Just Lather, That's All" by Hernando Tellez, portrays two political antagonists: a barber who is secretly the member of a revolutionary party and an officer in the army of an oppressive regime to which the barber is bitterly opposed. The author portrays the barber toying with the idea of slitting his political enemy's throat when the officer comes into his shop for a shave. But rather than taking sides, politically, Tellez uses his premise to demonstrate the irony of the situation, subtly exploring the risk-taking aspects of human experience.

5. What personal experiences and/or biases do you bring to the work?

The flip side of the author's bias is your own. You should not necessarily consider the world "bias" in this context a negative one. Rather, it is meant to denote your own perspective based upon your social, economic, and ethnic background. For example, if you are an African-American, and read the short story "Son in the Afternoon" by John Williams or *Ma Rainey's Black Bottom* by August Wilson, you are more likely to have a personal response based upon your racial heritage than if you are a white American.

Raising these questions (merely a sampling of the many you could ask) about what you read should demonstrate how literature challenges you, makes you wonder and question. True literature *requires* that you do this in order to derive full appreciation of it.

LEARNING TO ANALYZE LITERATURE

To illustrate, read the following two passages. The first is a fictive episode; the second is a very brief story entitled "Girl" by Jamaica Kincaid that you can find in your textbook. As you read the two passages, think about how they differ:

"You should be more tidy in your everyday habits," Janine's mother said sternly, as she examined her daughter's messy room.

Janine averted her eyes from her mother's severe gaze and uttered a deep sigh, as if to communicate that she had heard it all before.

"I want you to pay attention to me. I am your mother, and I set the rules for conduct in this house," her mother continued.

"Mother, why are you always lecturing me? The way I keep my room is my business. Patricia's mother lets her keep her room any way she likes. Besides that, she lets her stay out late, and gives her plenty of spending money." Janine was getting more and more frustrated.

Janine's mother was wishing her daughter would stop this endless comparison. She felt it undermined her authority.

"I'm not Patricia's mother. I'm your mother. And you're not Patricia, you're Janine, my daughter. Now I expect you to start following the rules around here."

• • •

Wash the white clothes on Monday and put them on the stone heap; wash the color clothes on Tuesday and put them on the clothesline to dry; don't walk barehead in the hot sun; cook pumpkin fritters in very hot sweet oil; soak your little cloths right after you take them off; when buying cotton to make yourself a nice blouse, be sure that it doesn't have gum on it, because that way it won't hold up well after a wash; soak salt fish overnight before you cook it; is it true that you sing benna[1] in Sunday school?; always eat your food in such a way that it won't turn someone else's stomach; on Sundays try to walk like a lady and not like the slut you are so bent on becoming; don't sing benna in Sunday school; you musn't speak to wharf-rat boys, not even to give directions; don't eat fruits on the street—flies will follow you; *but I don't sing benna on Sundays at all and never in Sunday school;* this is how to sew on a button; this is how to make a buttonhole for the button you have just sewed on; this is how to hem a dress when you see the hem coming down and so to prevent yourself from looking like the slut I know you are so bent on becoming; this is how you iron your father's khaki shirt so that it doesn't have a crease; this is how you iron your father's khaki pants so that they don't have a crease; this is how you grow okra—far from the house, because okra tree harbors red ants; when you are growing dasheen, make sure it gets plenty of water or else it makes your throat itch when you are eating it; this is how you sweep a corner; this is how you sweep a whole house; this is how you sweep a yard; this is how you smile to someone you don't like at all; this is how you smile to someone you like completely; this is how you set a table for tea; this is how you set a table for dinner; this is how you set a table for dinner with an important guest; this is how you set a table for lunch; this is how

---

[1] Calypso or rock and roll.

you set a table for breakfast; this is how to behave in the presence of men who don't know you very well, and this way they won't recognize immediately the slut I have warned you against becoming; be sure to wash every day, even if it is with spit; don't squat down to play marbles—you are not a boy, you know; don't pick people's flowers—you might catch something; don't throw stones at blackbirds, because it might not be a blackbird at all; this is how to make a bread pudding; this is how to make doukona; this is how to make pepper pot; this is how to make a good medicine for a cold; this is how to make a good medicine to throw away a child before it even becomes a child; this is how to catch a fish; this is how to throw back a fish you don't like, and that way something bad won't fall on you; this is how to bully a man; this is how a man bullies you; this is how to love a man, and if this doesn't work there are other ways, and if they don't work don't feel too bad about giving up; this is how to spit up in the air if you feel like it, and this is how to move quick so that it doesn't fall on you; this is how to make ends meet; always squeeze the bread to make sure it's fresh; *but what if the baker won't let me feel the bread?;* you mean to say that after all you are really going to be the kind of woman who the baker won't let near the bread?

Now ask yourself a few questions.

- Which of the two excerpts is more challenging to you, the reader?
- Which one is more intriguing and more original?
- Which one requires more thought, more *critical thinking?*
- Which requires a second reading?
- Which seems to have a unique style?
- Which has an authorial voice, something special that makes it stand out from other things you've read?

If you review the two selections, only "Girl" *requires* you to think in order to appreciate and understand it. For example, who is speaking and who is being spoken to in the second excerpt? In the first, it is all clear and obvious. The dialogue sounds familiar, and has probably been echoed in numerous stories to be found in magazines and in the drawers of would-be authors. In the second, however, things are not as transparent upon first glance. You must infer certain meanings based on what the author has provided in the way of tone, diction, and voice. In the first selection, the author is "telling" the reader how the character feels with such indicators as "Janine's mother said sternly" and "Janine was getting more and more frustrated." In the latter, the author is "showing" you. What is she showing? That is the key to the meaning of the short story. The fact that the story is written in the imperative mode, that its tone is stern, didactic, and commanding should indicate that the author is demonstrating what strategies are needed for survival among women who live in a specific culture, and how these strategies are transmitted from generation to generation. By figuring out how the speaker is feeling and what her relationship is to the person being spoken to, you arrive at an understanding of the selection.

Another critical issue an educated reader might pose is what *formal* aspects make "Girl" special. What is there about its style that sets it apart from other writing? For example, consider the issue of person. The latter excerpt is written in the second-person narrative or "you" form (implied but not stated since it is in the imperative mode). This in itself adds a bit of originality to the work, for it is probable that most if not all fiction you have read has been written in the first-person or "I" form, or the third-person or "he/she" form. (A complete discussion of this subject appears in the "point of view" section in Chapter 3.) But it is not enough merely to be original. You should also consider the purpose or effect of using the second person. Perhaps it provides a way for the writer to more directly imitate true conversation. If you compare the two excerpts, you will probably agree that the latter does seem to mirror the vibrant, continuous quality of speech, while the former seems a bit stilted and contrived, and perhaps worst of all, generic.

Yet another element of active reading is recognizing the author's use of language. Like spoken language, written language has rhythm, sound, tone, diction, imagery, and syntax. In the second selection, you may have noted the music-like quality of the speaker. This may be attributed to the Caribbean dialect and its intonations. For example, if you review the selection by Kincaid, you will notice the author employs such literary devices as alliteration (repetition of consonant sounds), assonance (repetition of vowel sounds), and inventive use of punctuation (the string of clauses held together by semicolons to keep up the movement of the language).

Originality, subtlety, concerns with the aesthetics of language: all three are good indicators that what you are reading is literature, and not just standard prose. Notable writers like Jamaica Kincaid are aware of and incorporate these aspects of language into their writing. And the more you read, think critically about, and write about literature, the more mastery you will acquire in identifying these and other components that enable literary artists to make significant and memorable statements about human experience.

DEVELOPING A CRITICAL PERSPECTIVE

The more you read literature, the easier it will be for you to spot those elements that are worthy of critical analysis and further study. If you read a poem, for example, you can base your reading and understanding of it on your past experience of thinking critically about texts you have already mastered. Reading the short poem "Wild Nights–Wild Nights!" by Emily Dickinson—after having read and analyzed "Girl"—should provide you with the skills to scrutinize and "decode" the poem as a more informed and educated reader. Take a few moments to read the "Wild Nights–Wild Nights!" in its entirety and reflect upon it:

Wild Nights–Wild Nights!

Were I with thee
Wild Nights should be
Our Luxury!

Futile–the Winds–
To a Heart in port–
Done with the Compass–
Done with the Chart–

Rowing in Eden–
Ah, the Sea!
Might I but move–Tonight–
In Thee!

Thinking critically about the poem should now come easier. You should be able to raise and answer for yourself questions of narrator, voice, style, language, and syntax. For an important aspect of being an educated reader is being able to ask appropriate questions on your own. You may ask yourself such things as what is the tone (emotional tenor) of the poem? Who is speaking? How is syntax used to contribute to the poem's effect? Note, for example, how Dickinson's use of dashes breaches the conventions of customary punctuation. Mentally rearrange the lines in a more typical way and compare the two renderings. What do you discover? Examine the phrase "Rowing in Eden." What does it imply? How does it fit into the overall message of the poem? What is the effect of the nautical imagery? It should be clear to you now that the more you know the method and "language" of literary criticism (a subject treated fully in Part Two of this text), the richer your experience of it will be, and the more discriminating a reader you will become. Ultimately, when the time comes to write about literature, you will have the critical tools necessary to forge your ideas and thoughts into a well-crafted essay.

WRITING ABOUT LITERATURE

Writing about literature adds a unique variable to the equation of an assignment for English class. In order to write about a poem, short story, novel, or play, you must read critically and understand the unique and peculiar aspects of literature. With such an understanding, the analysis, interpretation, and decoding of literature can become a more organized and often more rewarding activity for you.

When you write, you write for a reason or a purpose. The well-known British essayist, journalist, and novelist, George Orwell, addressed this issue in his famous essay, "Why I Write." In it, he enumerated the reasons he wrote. Among them were "the desire to seem clever," the "desire to share an experience which one feels is valuable and ought not to be missed," "to find out true facts," and the "desire to push the world in a certain direction." Perhaps the reason this essay has become a classic is that it articulates an important issue about writers themselves. Orwell was addressing the reason for and purpose of his own essays and fiction, but it may be just as fruitful to ask the same question of the type of writing you will be doing in this course (and perhaps in future courses and careers). While your motives for writing may not be as ambitious as Orwell's, an understanding of the purposes of writing about literature may help you address the challenge with more clarity and understanding.

Since the times of classical Greece, philosophers have created taxonomies to identify the various forms and purposes of writing. While these systems vary from theorist to theorist, the following list provides convenient categories and sample selections from your literature anthology to elucidate them.

Writing to Summarize

Summarizing requires that you distill the major aspects of a work of literature, for example, its theme, characterization, setting, tone, and the like. Summarizing is helpful in formulating what you believe to be the essential elements of what you have read, and communicating them to others. You may also think of summarizing as an exercise for the mind. It challenges you to think about and express succinctly what you have read. Thus, in writing an essay tracing the developments of African-American drama in the twentieth century, you might begin your discussion of *Ma Rainey's Black Bottom* to include its basic characters, setting, theme, tone, and mood. A summarizing paragraph might go something like this:

> *Ma Rainey's Black Bottom,* set in a makeshift recording studio during the 1930s, depicts the economic and artistic control of black artists by white producers through a series of vignettes that show the resentment felt by black musicians toward their employers and to each other, despite the fact that they have been selected to play backup for a leading singer of the period by the name of Ma Rainey. Their banter reveals feelings of oppression, hopelessness, self-deprecation, and desperation, and culminates in a violent and ultimately deadly confrontation between two of the musicians: one who advocates that the black man take greater control of his destiny; the other attempting to exploit the issue by devising music more to the white man's taste.

Writing to summarize is often an intermediate step in the writing process in that it can be a preparation to writing an essay comparing and contrasting different works of literature or classifying a particular work of literature for inclusion into a particular school or genre.

Writing to Respond Personally

Perhaps the very first way we responded to writing as children was emotionally, before we had criteria established for us as to *how* we were to respond or *what* we were to seek out in a text to respond to. When you respond personally, you are actually developing a thesis about what you have read, even if it is merely to demonstrate how you feel about a particular work of literature. Responding to a text personally puts you directly in touch with what affects you about a work of literature.

Writing to Analyze

Writing is a process where feedback plays a crucial role. When you analyze what you read, you can more succinctly express on paper the significance of what you have read. By the same token, writing itself often helps stimulate ideas that had not occurred to you or were existing in only an inchoate state. Writing to analyze often enables you to zero in on a particular aspect or feature of a work of literature. For example, reading, then writing an analysis of light imagery in the poem "There's a Certain Slant of Light" by Emily Dickinson can make the experience of reading and understanding the poem a more profound one. Like all forms of analysis, writing an analysis of a work of literature broadens and deepens your understanding.

Writing to Compare and Contrast

You gather knowledge about a field of inquiry through study. The more you study, the more you are likely to gain expertise in your field of endeavor. Comparing and contrasting works of literature is perhaps one of the most salient ways of developing your ability to discriminate between what is good and bad; understand what is unique about an author's work; and discern differences between authors, literary styles, genre, and different periods of literary history. You may compare many different aspects of literature. Perhaps the most fruitful forms of comparison are those that you spontaneously or instinctively become aware of through your reading. For instance, you may discover common themes between two poems, two short stories, or two plays, and to enrich your discovery, choose to write about what you see are the essential similarities and/or differences between the two. For example, two poems in your anthology, "Photograph of My Father in His Twenty-Second Year" and "My Papa's Waltz," relate the memory of a father by his son. Neither memory is positive, and much sadness and betrayal seem to be expressed by both authors toward their respective fathers. But on closer examination, Carver's portrait seems to have the more pathos and sympathy. Thus, in contrasting the two poems, you might generate a theme such as the following: "While both 'Photograph of My Father in His Twenty-Second Year' by Carver and 'My Papa's Waltz' by Roethke portray a father/son relationship absent of healthy emotional affiliation, Carver's portrait is the more tender, sympathetic, and kind." An essay which posited this thesis would be one that compares tone; however, comparison/contrast essays can also address style, ideology, theme, and culture.

Writing to Classify

You probably spend much of your waking life classifying: classifying types of professors, types of food, types of jobs, and so forth. The ability to classify is a vital part of your intelligence. It helps you to see connections, understand relationships, and hone your skills at discerning similarities and differences between people and objects. Classifying literature provides you with a means of organizing your readings and coming to conclusions about what you have read in terms of where it fits in to a particular style, genre, historical period, ideology, or theme. For example, your anthology is classified around genres: fiction, poetry, and drama. As an exercise in classification, see if you can derive a meaningful classification from some of the works you have read in your anthology. Remember, however, that there are innumerable ways to classify, but the fruitful ones provide you with a means of gaining insights and helping to appreciate more fully what you have read.

Writing to Present an Argument

When you see the term "argument" in a writing assignment, it usually means something similar to "prove" or "demonstrate." You do this in writing about literature through developing your main point, and then providing supporting evidence to prove your point. Presenting an argument when writing about literature is very similar to the way a lawyer argues a case in court. He or she presents the thesis—that his or her client is innocent—then provides the proof to demonstrate the truth of the argument. Take, for example, the short story, "The Lottery." Since its publication, critics and students have tackled its meaning through analyzing the nature of the community it depicts, the behavior of its characters, its setting, social relationships in the town, and other elements. Some critics say it demonstrates blind adherence to ritual, the evils of fascism, communism, and the deadly consequences of conservatism. Perhaps your reading of the story can provide a new argumentative approach.

Writing to Evaluate

You are probably familiar with writing that evaluates if you have ever read a movie review or a book review in your favorite paper or magazine. Many people turn to these reviews in helping them plan their entertainment if they feel they can safely rely on the judgment of the reviewer. When you write to evaluate, you are judging what you are reading. You are considering whether what you have read has merit or not. Evaluation, however, is a complex matter, and much personal bias goes into an evaluation. Perhaps the best way to write a competent evaluation of literature is to read as much of it as possible. For example, if you critically and carefully read one of the subsections in your anthology, you will probably come up with a few favorites. You can then return to these selections and ask yourself, "Why do I favor this selection over these others?" Writing to evaluate will help you understand what qualities are considered meritorious in literature, and at the same time help you understand yourself. Through analyzing which works of literature you prefer and why, you can discover your own literary tastes. Consider the following evaluation, for example: "'Big Bertha Stories' by Bobbie Anne Mason is an original, imaginative portrait of a Vietnam veteran's attempt to find coherence in a life that has had torment and pain." This statement has a thesis, but a thesis that is evaluative owing to the words "original" and "imaginative." To document this evaluation, the writer would then proceed to show through example how the work possesses these two positive attributes.

We shall continue to deal with some of these approaches in subsequent chapters. For now, it is important for you to know that writing about literature enjoys a long tradition. After all, Aristotle, the Greek philosopher, provided us with a study of dramatic literature in his *Poetics* over 2000 years ago. From the age of classic Greece to the present, we have been writing about literature. The concerns and approaches of literary critics and interpreters have been greatly influenced and shaped by the political, social, religious, and ideological forces of their times. Given these variables, we can agree that there is no single meaning in a text. When you read a text, you interact with it to create those meanings that you plan to write about.

APPROACHES TO LITERATURE

Thus far, you may have noticed that we have discussed literature in general and several works in particular by focusing on the works themselves. A school of literary criticism that had its roots in the 1920s and flourished in the 1950s, often referred to as "The New Criticism," popularized the approach of centering all meaning of a work of literature based on what was written on the page. But if you think for a moment, it should be obvious that there are many other ways to examine a poem, a short story, or a play. For example, you could examine the biographical elements of a work of literature by studying the writer's life. Or, if you're interested in the works of Freud or Jung or Lacan, you might apply a psychological perspective to a work, trying to understand, perhaps, the unconscious meanings of a play or story. For example, the poem "Adolescence-II" by Rita Dove contains images that seem to have been uncovered from deep within the psyche. Actually, for the past quarter of a century, many approaches to studying and thinking critically about literature have emerged. Some have remained popular; others have diminished in their influence. Nevertheless, a brief cross section of these various methods can enrich the way you look at literature and expand the ways you think about it. The following summary is provided to give you a taste of these different methods. If any of them intrigue you, it is easy to follow up your interest by asking your instructor or by referring to the literary criticism of your library.

Psychological Criticism

You are probably familiar with the concept of interpreting dreams. You may relate a dream to a close friend, and together try to figure out what the symbolism might signify. This activity is similar to the methods used in psychological criticism. This form of criticism attempts to apply modern psychological theories, primarily Freudian (and more recently Lacanian), to understanding literature. There are various ways that you may critique a work of literature from a psychological perspective. As noted above, you may take a work that has obvious symbolism and interpret what each image means. Another use of psychological criticism in literature is to attempt to understand the underlying motivations of a character in a short story or novel. What are the unconscious wishes of the women in the short story "A House of Flesh" by Yussef Idriss or "Astronomer's Wife" by Kay Boyle? Or what desires lie hidden in the adolescent relationships between the teenagers in Alice Munro's "The Found Boat" or in James Joyce's "Araby"? Another story in the anthology that lends itself to psychological criticism is "Big Bertha Stories" by Bobbie Anne Mason. What psychological function do these stories serve for the burned-out Vietnam vet? Psychological criticism has also proved fruitful in examining so-called "stream of consciousness" writing, where we purportedly are entering into the mind of a literary work's narrator, as for example, we seem to do in the poem in this anthology "The Love Song of J. Alfred Prufrock" by T.S. Eliot. Authors who have used this device in novels include such notables as James Joyce, Virginia Woolf, and William Faulkner. A third function of psychological criticism may be to understand an author's psyche through a study of his or her works. For example, many critics claim you can infer Hemingway's psychological makeup by reading his stories. If you have read "A Clean, Well-Lighted Place," what sort of man would you believe had written it, and what are his values?

Historical Criticism

Historical criticism attempts to study literature by placing it within the context of the time in which it was written. Thus, styles and forms of writing may be historically based. Much of Shakespearean drama is written in blank verse, as in *Othello*. However, you would be hardpressed to find a contemporary play written in verse today. Most likely, we would think the author was being either old-fashioned or naive. Content as well as style is greatly influenced by historical forces. If you read Matthew Arnold's "Dover Beach" without a knowledge of the changes in European culture at the turn of the twentieth century, you cannot hope to understand many of the poem's references. The same holds true for

Yeats' "Easter 1916." You must not only be aware of the Irish Liberation Movement to appreciate the poem, but you must have some inkling of the personages referred to throughout the poem.

The New Historicism

New Historicist critics take the concept of history and give it a new perspective. These critics argue that indeed literature can be studied from a historical point of view, but you must be careful not to inject your own historical perspective into a text that was written in another century. For example, the issues of jealousy raised in *Othello,* the issues of incest raised in *Oedipus Rex,* or the issues of the American dream addressed in *Death of a Salesman* may seem familiar and obvious to us. They might appear typical subjects for an afternoon TV show, in fact. However, the significance of the themes in these plays must be considered within the context of the time they were written. *Death of a Salesman,* for example, opened the eyes of a generation to the reductionist, distorted view that the goal in life was to make a good impression on others, and to the need to make as much money as possible to prove your self-worth.

Biographical Criticism

Biographical criticism bears some similarities to historical criticism, only its concerns focus more on the particular life of the author, rather than the time he or she was writing in. Knowing that Wilfred Owen witnessed the horrors of World War I can help us understand the motivation behind the subject matter and themes in his poems, for example, the two contained in this anthology, "Anthem for Doomed Youth" and "Dulce et Decorum Est." Many poems cry out for biographical understanding of the author, for example Raymond Carver's poem "Photograph of My Father in His Twenty-Second Year" or Sylvia Plath's "Daddy" or Dylan Thomas's "Fern Hill." Prose fiction too lends itself to biographical criticism, as with "A Conversation With My Father" by Grace Paley or "Girl" by Jamaica Kincaid. This is not to suggest that a work of fiction is a direct transcription of an author's life, but many authors use their experiences as sources of their richest work.

Marxist and Social Criticism

Although the philosopher Karl Marx wrote his major works in the nineteenth century, many literary critics have used his analysis of class conflict to examine even the earliest forms of literature. Perhaps because issues of class conflict seem to have existed at all times in human history (there were strong class divisions among the Greeks, for example), and since literature is often about people in conflict with one another and with society-at-large, Marxist criticism lends itself quite readily to explanations of much literature. Although issues of race and ethnicity are implicated in many of the stories in this anthology, many can simultaneously be interpreted using a Marxist paradigm. Even if the theories of Marx are not applied directly, the importance of power between and among individuals and groups, and the powerful influences of the conventions of society over our behavior tend to have at least some relevance to a Marxist reading. Richard Wright's "The Man Who Was Almost a Man" subtly shows the potentially insidious effects of class and racism on the future of one young man. More obviously and graphically, Nadine Gordimer's "The Train from Rhodesia" and "A Summer Tragedy" by Arna Bontemps can be read as studies in the effects of sanctioned economic inequality.

Structuralism

The literary method of structuralism takes its inspiration from the work of Ferdinand de Saussure, a Swiss linguist whose major ideas were transcribed by his students at the beginning of the twentieth century. The basic thesis of structuralism is that language is a system, a code of communication with its own rules and regulations. For example, sentences in English have a particular syntax which, if broken, ruptures the sense of the language. Literary critics have taken this basic idea and applied it to literature, primarily in their attempt to raise the importance of genre as an explanatory principle in discussing works of literature. For example, a structuralist might read a detective story, and rather than discuss merits of the style or the symbolic significance of the locale, use the story as a tool to understand the conventions of detective story type. Therefore, structuralist critics are often interested in examining works of literature to understand literature as a whole. So, for example, reading "The South" by Borges, a structuralist might be more interested in discussing the concept of initiation and relating this concept to other works where initiation plays a significant role. Many advocates of structuralism have claimed that the idea of quality in literature must be reconsidered. Rather than ask whether a poem or story or play is well-written, the question a structuralist might ask is "how well does this work of fiction fulfill the conventions of the genre it is a member of?"

Reader-Response Criticism

If a tree falls in the forest and no ones sees or hears it, has it really fallen? This old riddle bears considerable significance to the school of reader-response criticism. People who advocate this approach to literature claim that a play or story or poem only exists in its relationship to the reader. Without the reader, it is not literature. The one who reads fulfills an essential aspect of the literary process. While this may seem rather obvious, reader-response criticism was an important reaction to the strong tendency of some critics—particularly the New Critics mentioned earlier—to consider the text in isolation, as though it were an immutable thing whose essence could be uncovered if one simply had the right tools and perspicuity. But reader-response critics hold that we construct meanings from what we read based upon our own individual experience, our cultural background, and the "community" within which we operate. You are a college student, for example, and you constitute with your peers a community. Your study of literature is obviously being influenced by the views that the academic community holds in so far as the way literature should be examined. Even your class itself may have its own biases toward interpretation (most likely controlled by the instructor or perhaps the philosophical perspective of your English department). That a text is incomplete in itself, and that reading it makes it come to life, gives more power to the reader, and some reader-response critics place as much if not more importance on the role of the reader as they do that of the author. Suppose, for example, your father works as a traveling salesman. This may have quite a bearing on your response to the play *Death of a Salesman*. Your response to any of the selections in the anthology may be strongly determined by your own class, racial, and ethnic background. Or take something even more basic: your gender. Chances are that male and female students may see a work of literature quite differently. After reading the story "The Lady with the Pet Dog" by Chekhov, your focus on character might be a result of how you identify with the characters, and that identification may well be based on your sex.

Feminist Criticism

Feminist criticism is an outgrowth of the feminist movement that began in the 1960s, but has been used retroactively to examine works wherein gender issues are prominent. In fact, feminist critics often uncover issues of gender in older texts that previously may not have been considered literature that had feminist implications. One major and legitimate complaint of feminist critics has been that women writers have been ignored since it has been mainly men who have ruled on what is considered literature and what is not. Feminist critics have adopted many writers that have lived in obscurity, so that today authors like Kate Chopin and Charlotte Perkins Gilman and Zora Neale Hurston have been recognized as major writers where formerly their works went unread. Feminist critics often look for and find themes of women's oppression, and stories such as "Astronomer's Wife," "A Respectable Women," and "Roselily" are seen as works that not only examine women's lives but advocate for them.

INTERPRETING LITERATURE

In a class full of literature students, there is a strong possibility that there will be many interpretations of the same literary work. At the same time, the teacher's interpretation may differ from the students'. Who determines which is the correct interpretation? Or is it safe to say that there is more than one correct interpretation? Literature is open to so many readings, interpretations, and opinions that readers seldom agree on *every* aspect of a literary work. One may say that there are various competent readings, but not *all* readings are valid. You may even change your mind over an interpretation of a particular poem or story depending on when you read it, how often, and in what context.

Regardless of your personal interpretation of a story, it is most probable that the more carefully you read a work of literature, the more likely your interpretation will be valid. If you believe you understand the theme of a work, the particulars of it must back up your comprehension of it. The theme or meaning of a work is a generalization; the elements in it are the particulars. Put another way, your interpretation of a theme is your argument; its various elements are your proofs. If the proofs don't follow, then chances are you have a weak argument.

Some works are easier to interpret than others, however. The play *Krapp's Last Tape,* for example, has been analyzed, studied, debated, and interpreted over and over. On the other hand, a play like *Suppressed Desires* is fairly direct in its presentation of its theme, and few major arguments over its meaning are likely to be forthcoming. There are quite a few factors that influence the difficulty of interpretation of a work of literature. Two major ones are the degree to which the work breaks the conventions of genre; the other is the degree to which the motivations and/or the actions of a character are ambiguous. There have been many classroom arguments over whether the main character in Richard Wright's "The Man Who Was Almost a Man" actually becomes a man by escaping the provincial town he is living in or whether he is merely running away from his problems and therefore remaining a boy.

EVALUATING LITERATURE

"That was a really good movie!" "I couldn't stand the play we read in class." "I hate poetry." These common assertions are all evaluations. However, they are not particularly articulate ones. To evaluate or judge a work of literature requires that you have a set of guidelines. Guidelines for evaluation are not etched in stone, and depending upon your philosophical bent, can vary greatly. For example, a social critic might evaluate a work of literature depending upon whether it reflects the individual's own world view. If you've gone to the movies and have seen the "good guys" win, you may decide it's a good movie because it ended the way you wanted it to or anticipated.

In most English classes, however, evaluation is usually focused on the integrity of the work itself:

• Do all the elements seem to fit together in a cohesive unit?
• Do the characters seem plausible?
• Are the language, tone, and diction consistent, or if they aren't has the author provided a good reason for the inconsistency?

- Does the work seem to have an original voice, or like the example of "Janine and her Mother," does it seem to be generic?
- Are the ideas in the work consistent?
- Does each element seem to contribute to the overall theme?
- Is the language vivid, appropriate, and accurate for what the author is trying to convey?

These are only some of the questions you should ask yourself when evaluating literature. For example, if you read the poems by Langston Hughes in this anthology, ask yourself whether their diction and tone seem to ring true. Perhaps one way to summarize these questions about evaluation is to ask yourself the question, "Does the author of this work seem to have an intimate grasp of the universe of the poem or story or play?"

The more you read and ask questions like these, the more you will develop your own evaluative skills, and not have to rely on the views of others. We will return to these issues of interpretation and evaluation in several subsequent chapters.

2

The Writing Process

Reading literature and writing about it are two closely related processes, so much so that the skilled reader of literature should always read with a pencil in hand, and mark the text in order better to understand it. (If you are working with a library book, make a photocopy of the material so that you can mark it without destroying someone else's book!) In literature, language is often compressed, or squeezed tightly into a shape or *genre* (meaning kind or type). Reading with a pencil is a tool that helps you to separate gently the layers of meaning. The process of writing about literature helps you to examine these layers one at a time in a formal and disciplined way so that your reading can be shared with others. In this unit we will look at the steps a reader takes in order to become a writer.

HIGHLIGHTING AND ANNOTATING THE TEXT

Let's take as an example the short story by Jamaica Kincaid, "Girl." The first step is to *read* the piece through at least twice. Next, read with a pencil. As you read, use the pencil to:

1. Circle key words (words that you do not understand, words that are repeated, for instance).
2. Underline lines or phrases that relate to the theme of the chapter, in this case children and families.
3. Annotate by asking questions in the margin about what the writer means or to record your own responses to the writer's words.

— simple, domestic task

(this is how) to (sew) on a button; (this is how)   *repeated phrase*
to make a (button)hole for the button you have
just (sewed) on; (this is how) to (hem) a dress   *rhythm of repetition*
when you see the (hem) coming down and so to   *— unusual word!*
who is prevent yourself from looking like the [slut] I   *who is the "S"?*
you? know you are so bent on becoming; . . .

4. Highlight key phrases: "this is how" is repeated, so it might be important; the word "slut" seems powerful and stands out; related words like "sew" and "button," "buttonhole," and "hem" tell what the speaker is talking about.

You should read the entire story in this way, circling new words like "benna" and "dasheen."

Next, use a dictionary or a glossary to find the meanings of words you do not know. The word "slut," for instance, appears in the *Oxford English Dictionary* with several meanings, including:

"A woman of a low or loose character; a bold or impudent girl; a hussy, a jade."

Where would you look for the definition of words like "benna" and "dasheen" if these were not in your standard American dictionary?

TAKING NOTES

Once you have carefully read the work several times, and highlighted and annotated as much as you can, the next step is to begin taking notes to help organize your impressions of the work so you can develop a *thesis* for your essay.

Notes can include:

- Listing
- Asking Questions
- Brainstorming
- Developing Subject Trees
- Keeping a Journal

Listing

Listing is the most familiar technique for organizing thoughts. We all make shopping lists or lists of friends to invite to a party or names for sending out Christmas cards. When writing about literature, the list might help put ideas into categories. If your subject were "Girl," you might begin with a "do" list and a "don't" list:

Do: wash clothes on certain days, cook fritters in oil; sew buttons on; walk like a lady; love a man.

Don't: speak to ''wharf-rat'' boys; walk like a slut; pick other people's flowers; be the kind of woman the baker won't let squeeze the bread.

Or you could list whatever has struck you as significant in your reading, and then review and evaluate what you have listed to see if any common theme has emerged.

Here is a typical list generated by one student on her notebook computer.

1. The imperative tone of the story shows a rigid system of parental authority in place, nothing like modern families in America today.
2. Many of the specific references in the story indicate the presence of a particular West Indian culture, for example, ''pumpkin fritters,'' ''don't sing benna,'' ''wharf-rat boys,'' ''dasheen,'' ''doukona,'' etc.
3. The cultural milieu is one in which the types of directives the mother presents to the daughter are traditional female ones involving such activities as cooking, sewing, cleaning, housekeeping, and so on.
4. The mother also displays a traditional set of values by trying to instill in her daughter the proper comportment to assume around men.
5. Folklore and superstition are also replete in the lore which the mother is transmitting to the daughter, providing further evidence of a traditional culture; for example, she instructs her ''how to throw back a fish you don't like,'' ''don't throw stones at blackbirds,'' ''how to spit up in the air if you feel like it.''
6. Religion is another significant cultural value which the mother tries to instill in her daughter; for example, she says ''on Sundays try to walk like a lady,'' ''don't sing benna in Sunday school.''
7. Above all, the mother displays the typical attitude of any mother who lives in a traditional culture and whose role it is to instill in her daughter the conventions and mores of her culture.

The function of listing is to generate ideas that ultimately can be used to help you organize the first draft of your essay.

Asking Questions

What pattern do the lists reveal? What insight into the story's meaning do the ''do'' and ''don't'' lists offer? The next step is to ask more questions, including who, what, and why.

Who is speaking in the story ''Girl''?
Whom is she/he speaking to?
How do we know?
Why are the sentences so long?
What is the tone of the speaker's voice?
Why are there so many domestic details, about food and behavior?
Are there any clues to the gender of the speaker, and the listener?
Does the language limit the story to one time or place, or is it universal in its meaning?
Does this work remind me of any others that I have read?

Brainstorming

Brainstorming is another way to generate ideas for a paper. Brainstorming can be done by yourself, but it can also be done in a group with two or three students who have all read the same story or poem.

- Sit in a small group.
- Have one member of the group read the story or poem out loud.
- Then let everyone offer his or her own insights into the meaning of the poem.
- Assign one member to record all of the responses.

Your brainstorming might result in a page that looks like this:

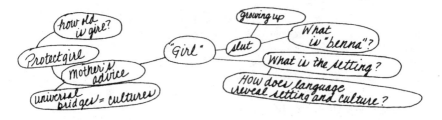

Working with a group, you may find that the ideas of other classmates, whose backgrounds are different from your own, help you identify special features of the story you might have overlooked.

Developing Subject Trees

Developing subject trees is another way to think about the story. From the ''trunk'' of the story ''Girl,'' you might branch out into topics:

a mother's advice to her daughter
women's writing
do's and don'ts about sex
domestic details
unusual language: how does the writer convey cultural identity through details and local
    language?
etiquette books; Dear Abby; Miss Manners; giving advice: how is the mother's monologue
    like a ''Dear Abby'' letter?

Keeping a Journal

Keeping a journal is another way to record your ideas about a work of literature. You can use pages in a looseleaf, or keep a separate notebook. Each time you read a new story, start a new page and jot down your impressions of the work. Let yourself use all of the techniques—listing, asking questions, brainstorming and subject trees—to record your impressions. You will find that when you want to write a paper, glancing back at journal entries makes finding a topic easier. A journal page might look like this:

> A mother seems to be speaking to her daughter about all sorts of chores and different kinds of behavior. What to do and what not to do is the subject. The mother talks nonstop. It's as if she is giving the "girl" a lifetime of advice in one lecture. I can almost see the mother: maybe she's hanging clothes on a line in the hot sun and the daughter, she's about twelve, is following holding a basket of clothespins. The two work together and the mother talks as she hangs the sheets. I say the girl is about twelve because the mother uses the word "slut," so she's already worried about her daughter hanging out with boys and getting into trouble. What's funny is that even though it sounds like the mother is just rambling, when I read the story again, it was like there was a rhythm to it, and a whole lifetime of experience. I don't know what "benna" is, but whatever it is, the mother doesn't seem to like it much.

SELECTING AND LIMITING THE TOPIC

Once you have read the work, discussed it with your teacher and classmates, highlighted, annotated, and taken lots of notes, you are ready to find a topic for your essay.

One way to select a topic is to ask questions and then write out a tentative answer. You can use the questions you asked while taking notes, and expand these with key words from the brainstorming session and the journal entry.

Who is speaking, to whom, about what?
The mother gives her daughter womanly advice.
Possible topic: something about mother-daughter relationships.

Once you have some ideas, the next step is to narrow the topic, or limit it, so that it is manageable in an essay of about 500 to 750 words. Some inexperienced writers think that keeping the topic very broad, like "women writers," makes it easier to write because they won't run out of material. But more experienced writers know better. The more you can limit the topic, the easier it is to support and organize the essay.

Broad topic: Women writers
More limited: Women writers' use of details
Even more limited: use of domestic details by African-American women writers

Once you have a sufficiently limited topic, you can begin to plan and write the essay, using the following steps:

- Developing a Thesis
- Considering Audience and Purpose
- Revising and Editing
- Submitting the Final Manuscript

DEVELOPING A THESIS

Developing a thesis means that you have to decide what you want to say about the limited topic. The *thesis* is the most important part of the essay, for the thesis controls the plan for what follows. The thesis gives the reader your point of view or opinion on the limited topic. It may also suggest which strategy you plan to use to organize the body of the essay.

If your limited topic is use of domestic detail by African-American women writers, you can create a thesis by asking, what do I want to say about this topic? What do I mean? What is my purpose in writing the essay?

You can begin, as you did earlier, by asking questions.

Why am I interested in this topic?
What is unique or special about it?
What did I think about when I read the story that led me to this topic?
Do I like the story? Why or why not?
What about the story relates to the theme of children and families, and how does the story reflect on the multicultural themes of the other readings?

Sample thesis statements:

1. In her story "Girl," Jamaica Kincaid uses an accumulation of domestic details to reveal a mother's strict but loving concern for her daughter.
2. The mother in Jamaica Kincaid's story "Girl" cannot speak directly of her love for her daughter, so she uses details about a woman's everyday life to convey her pride and anxiety about her daughter.

Statements can be refined and expanded as you develop your ideas. The next step is to consider your audience and purpose.

CONSIDERING AUDIENCE AND PURPOSE

Who is my audience? In that way will knowing who the audience is shape my essay?
Why am I writing the essay? How will my purpose help me to choose a strategy for outlining the essay?

Your immediate audience is the instructor and your fellow students. At the same time, you are writing for a wider audience, the educated common reader, which might include anyone who has read Kincaid's story and wants to understand it better. Since your audience is a college audience, your writing will have a more formal tone than it might if you were merely having a conversation about the story with a friend. This tone is connected to the *purpose* of the essay. One purpose in writing is to help yourself analyze your own thoughts about the story by putting them down in writing. Another purpose, however, is to train yourself in a particular discipline, in the skill of college-level expository prose. By writing about literature in a college course, you are learning the conventions, or the rules and practices, of the world of professional writers. You are polishing your formal language skills and your skills in thinking and analysis in preparation for whatever career you will choose. Writing about literature, then, requires planning and attention to detail.

You can begin, once you have read the story, annotated it, taken notes, limited the topic and developed a thesis, and considered audience and purpose, to write the first draft.

WRITING AND REVISING

In order to write the draft, you can start with a simple outline:

Introduction, with thesis
Body paragraphs, with quotations from the story to support the thesis, normally using one of four major types discussed in the previous chapter: personal, analytical, comparative, or argumentative
Conclusion

In order to develop the body, you can decide which essay plan is best suited to the thesis.

- Is this a *personal essay?*
- Is this an *analytical essay?*
- Is this a *comparative essay?*
- Is this an *argumentative essay?*

Types of Essays

Read each sample essay and examine the writer's techniques. Then you will be ready to decide which strategy is best for the essay you want to write.

Personal As mentioned in Chapter 1, this type of essay allows the writer to speak in her own voice, and to relate the literature to her own experience. The essay may use analysis or argument, but the focus is on the personal. For instance, a personal essay on "Girl" might be written by an African-American woman who grew up in Barbados and moved to New York, and who identifies with the experience in the story now that she is raising her own daughter. In writing her draft, this student can talk about "Girl" by connecting Kincaid's story with her own life. Or, as in the sample essay that follows, the student uses his own voice to record his impressions of Elizabeth Bishop's poem, "Filling Station."

Sample Essay: Personal

Cars and traveling by car have been part of the American identity since the first car rolled off an assembly line. To many ears, the names of cars are a genre of American poetry: Mustang, Firebird, Impala, Thunderbird, Dart, Seville, Imperial, Galaxy, Eagle, New Yorker. I always wished I could get a job dreaming up names for new models of cars. It's probably not hard to explain why a poem called "Filling Station," by Elizabeth Bishop, made me nostalgic for the days before gas stations became hygienic self-service supermarts without any style or poetry.

"Filling Station" is a description of an old-fashioned gas station, family run, where grease and oil are soaked into every surface. The poem begins with the speaker at a distance, horrified at what it looks like: "Oh, but it is dirty!" is the first line. The speaker, probably a woman, notes that this is a "little" filling station, "oil-soaked, oil-permeated," sounding worried, as if *she* will be the one required to scrub out the petroleum stains with their "over-all black translucency."

In the second stanza, the speaker zooms in on the human scene, noting that the station is family run, as "Father wears a dirty,/oil-soaked monkey suit" and "several quick and saucy/and greasy sons assist him" in running the family business.

Seeing the individuals, the speaker begins to change her tune, to ask human questions about the place such as "Do they live in the station?" Does the "dirty dog" on the greasy wicker furniture suggest family life?

In the fourth stanza, more domestic details emerge, as if the speaker is like a photographer with a zoom lens. We see "Some comic books," "a big dim doily" and a "big hirsute begonia." The "little" station of the first stanza is growing rapidly! The black and white of the earlier stanzas is gradually being filled in with color and texture. The "hirsute" or hairy begonia is almost human in its itchy skin.

The fifth stanza is filled with questions:

Why the extraneous plant?
Why the taboret?
Why, oh why, the doily?
(Embroidered in daisy stitch
with marguerites, I think,
and heavy with gray crochet.)

The details, especially of the embroidery, imply that the speaker, no longer distant, has zoomed right up close, so close she can count the stitches on the doily, examine the crochet border. She is no longer in her car; she has entered the space, and the closeness provides a new worldview and answers to her questions:

Somebody embroidered the doily,
Somebody waters the plant,
. . .
Somebody loves us all.

This poem is about America. Beginning with the image of the filling station seen at a distance, the poem presents us with the outsider's view of the place: dirty, worn, gray, taken over by technology ("high-strung automobiles") and hopelessness. But, as the speaker moves in closer, the scene takes on color and human form. Family emerges, first in the visible father and sons, and, in a more subtle way, the invisible mark of the women folk, the embroidery, and the flowers. The speaker, once cynical and unseeing, learns to see more carefully and to interpret what she sees. The new vision is a small epiphany: somebody loves us all!

In the modern America of Edsel failures and Pinto disasters, "Filling Station" is not a nostalgic poem. It is a joyous personal expression of faith in human nature to survive the blackest oil pollution. Even if the doily is gray and dingy, the carefully stitched daisies are in bloom.

Analytical   This is a more commonly required type of essay. Here, you are asked to analyze, or closely examine, some aspect of the story or poem or play. What are the particular literary techniques the writer has used, such as metaphors or similes? What themes emerge in the text? The sample essay is an analysis of Theodore Roethke's poem, "My Papa's Waltz."

Sample Essay: Analytical

Theodore Roethke's poem, "My Papa's Waltz," shows that even the most difficult parent is the object of a child's love. By careful use of point of view, Roethke presents a scene from childhood as a drunken father comes home to an angry wife and a loving child. Careful analysis of the language reveals that Roethke gives us the scene not exactly as the child sees it at the time, but as he, now grown up, remembers it.

The point of view is announced in the title, when the word "papa" is used instead of "father." This informal word alerts us that the language is that of a person familiar with the subject.

In the first stanza, we are abruptly presented with the problem:

The whiskey on your breath
Could make a small boy dizzy;

We immediately share the speaker's dilemma of meeting the drunken father as he comes home. The next two lines of the stanza prevent us from fearing harm as we learn of the speaker's determination to hang on "like death" as his father picks him up and dances around the kitchen with him. "Such waltzing was not easy" can be taken in the literal sense, it was hard to hang on, and in the metaphoric sense, that "such waltzing," that is, such a situation, was "not easy."

In the second stanza, we meet the other grown up, the mother, who, in the child's view, "Could not unfrown" herself, as she watches her drunken husband cavorting "until the pans/Slid from the kitchen shelf." The mother, however, is seen only at a distance. The child's concern, his memory, is of the father, whose presence is so special: even if he is drunk he provides a good time. The mother's inability to "unfrown" her face suggests she has seen such behavior before and no longer finds it amusing.

The third stanza introduces a hint of violence, revealing the father's hand "battered on one knuckle" and the boy, pressed so hard against his father's body that "every step you missed/My ear scraped on a buckle." These small details, the battered knuckle, the iron buckle, imply a tough father, prone to fighting, for whom even the pleasure of a game with his son carries a threat of danger, of pain.

In the last stanza, the boy is carried off to bed by his father. We learn more through the seemingly simple observations of the speaker; the father's hand is "caked with dirt," suggesting he is a working-class father who makes his money by manual labor. Like the bruise and the buckle of the previous stanza, the word "beat" can refer to the waltz rhythm, but also carries a suggestion of violence, as if the son might be beaten at any moment if the play turns to anger. The last line is powerful, implying that for all the fear and violence, the son loves his father. As he is waltzed off to bed he is "Still clinging" to his papa's shirt.

The language when we first read "My Papa's Waltz" seems simple and direct, as if the child is really telling it as it happens. Upon rereading, however, we realize how compact and loaded with meaning the images are, suggesting that far from being spontaneous, they are thoughtfully being reconstructed by a much older son who is remembering his father from a distance. The last line tells us, most of all, that even at this distance, he is "clinging," if not to the shirt, then to the recollection of a father who may have been rough, but was, after all, the only father he had.

Comparative The comparative essay selects at least two works of literature, and begins with a thesis that shows a relationship between them. The body of the essay compares and contrasts the two (or more) works on the basis of three or four key points that are set out in the thesis. For instance, a student compares "Girl" and Gloria Naylor's "Kiswana Browne" on the basis of what they say about mother-daughter relationships. The student looks for similarities and also differences in the two works.

Sample Essay: Comparative

The relationship between mothers and daughters is a recurrent theme in stories by women, particularly African-American women writers in the twentieth century. For Gloria Naylor and Jamaica Kincaid, description of domestic life serves as a kind of code language for showing how two very different pairs of women come to terms with who they are, and how much they love one another.

Naylor's story "Kiswana Browne" is about a young woman who has changed her middle-class name of Melanie to Kiswana, and is trying to find her identity by moving into her own apartment in a run-down section of town not too far from the well-to-do suburb of Linden Hills where her mother still lives. One day, Kiswana looks out the window and sees her mother about to arrive for an unannounced visit. Her first reaction is shock: "'Oh, God, it's Mama'" she exclaims. The daughter's mind immediately turns to the domestic details of the apartment, which her mother has never seen before. First, she "gave silent thanks that the elevator was broken" because this gives her a few extra minutes to clean up. As she races around putting things away, we learn something about her lifestyle: "She rushed to the sofa bed and hastily closed it without smoothing the rumpled sheets and blanket or removing her nightgown. She felt that somehow the tangled bedcovers would give away the fact that she had not slept alone last night." From this bit of detail, we can see that Kiswana, alias Melanie, feels guilty about having an affair with Abshu, and feels she has to hide the evidence of her activity from her mother. She continues to scurry around: "She took up his shaving cream and razor and threw them into the bottom drawer of her dresser beside her diaphragm. Mama wouldn't dare pry into my drawers right in front of me, she thought as she slammed the drawer shut. Well, at least not the *bottom* drawer. She may come up with some sham excuse for opening the top drawer, but never the bottom one." Through these homey details, Naylor lets us learn a lot about Kiswana's rebellion from her middle-class parents. We learn that she has a lover with an African name, just as she has changed her own name to create a new identity. She is sleeping with him in her own apartment, trying to make it without help from her parents, even though this means living in a shabby building without much furniture. Her reaction to the sight of her mother, as revealed in the details of the dresser drawer, the tangled sheets, the shaving cream and the diaphragm, however, tells us that Kiswana is still a little bit afraid of her mother. Since she thinks her mother might still peek into the top drawer of the dresser, it seems as if she is saying that her mother still has control over her. Toward the end of the story, after she and her mother have had a long argument about politics, Kiswana "closed the door and turned around" and "spotted an envelope sticking between the cushions of her couch." Her mother has slipped her seventy-five much needed dollars. Kiswana is about to call out to her mother, but instead she changes her mind and "sat down in the chair with a long sigh . . . ." Just as she had hidden the diaphragm, her mother has hidden the envelope. In claiming it, and not calling her mother back, Kiswana demonstrates that she and her mother, for all their differences, are linked. Neither character says so directly, but the drawers and sheets and couch cushions tell the feelings in their own way, like a secret language between the two of them.

Similarly, Kincaid's story "Girl" uses domestic details to show another relationship between a mother and a daughter. Unlike Naylor's women, however, who are in a city, Kincaid's pair is in a rural setting. Instead of seeing events through the eyes of the daughter, this time we see them mostly from the mother's point of view. Kincaid's story does not use the third-person narrative Naylor's does, but is told in an unusual second-person voice. "Wash the white clothes on Monday" the story begins, and the reader has to figure out for herself what is going on. "Cook pumpkin fritters in very hot sweet oil; soak your little cloths

right after you take them off . . . .'' At first it all seems a jumble. We find, however, that like Naylor, Kincaid is piling up domestic details and asking us to think
about them as we figure out that the narrator is a mother speaking to her daughter: ''this is how to sew on a button; this is how to make a buttonhole for the
button you have just sewed on; this is how to hem a dress when you see the hem
coming down and so to prevent yourself from looking like the slut I know you
are so bent on becoming . . . .'' It is at the word ''slut'' that we realize there is
something about this mother-daughter relationship that reminds us of Kiswana
and her mother. It's as if, in the little girl, we have Kiswana at a young age, and
in the mother instructing her daughter, a reflection of the younger Mrs. Browne.
''Slut'' is a powerful word, suggesting according to the *Oxford English Dictionary,* ''a woman of low or loose character.'' The sewing on of the button, like all
of the other domestic duties, is provided almost as if to stop the girl from growing up to be a ''slut,'' as the mother might see Kiswana later on. The domestic
chores are supposed to keep the girl busy and out of trouble.

     If the two stories are different in these ways, they share a common theme
nevertheless. In the end, Kiswana's mother tucks the envelope between the sofa
cushions; the girl's mother ends by saying, ''you mean to say that after all you
are really going to be the kind of woman who the baker won't let near the
bread?'' Clearly, both mothers are proud of their daughters, even if they cannot
say so directly. The envelope to help pay the rent supports Kiswana's move toward independence, and perhaps makes her feel silly about the bottom drawer.
The girl's mother's reference to the baker makes clear that she, too, wants a
daughter who can stand up for herself and assert her independence. Both mothers,
through their domestic language, overcome the generation gap and express love
and understanding for their daughters.

Argumentative   This essay aims to persuade the reader to share your opinion
or interpretation of the literary work. The sample essay on Randall Jarrell's ''The
Death of the Ball Turret Gunner'' and Wilfred Owen's ''Dulce et Decorum Est''
argues for the inhumanity of war.

Sample Essay: Argumentative

     Wilfred Owen died in 1918, just as World War I ended; Randall Jarrell
was born in 1914, just as the war that killed Owen had begun. Both are poets
who argue eloquently against simplistic ideas of patriotism. Randall Jarrell's
poem, ''The Death of the Ball Turret Gunner'' is only five lines long, but it
presents one of the most impassioned antiwar statements of modern times. When
we read it alongside Wilfred Owen's ''Dulce et Decorum Est,'' a poem written in
the first world war, we can only conclude that even the best poets are helpless
when it comes to stopping the insanity of war.

"Dulce et Decorum Est" argues through powerful sensual images to persuade the folks back home not to accept propagandist descriptions of what it was like to be a soldier on the front lines. Owen uses irony to get his point across, especially with his title. "Dulce et Decorum Est" comes from a Latin poet and means "It is sweet and fitting." The rest of the line comes at the end of the poem, "to die for one's country." At the beginning of the poem, the reader might assume the speaker is taking the expected patriotic stance, as Horace did, arguing for the necessity of war. By the end of the poem, we are persuaded otherwise. Each section of the poem focuses our attention on one of the five senses, so that we experience the war in all its brutality. We *see* the horror of men "Bent double, like old beggars under sacks/Knock-kneed" as they march asleep on their feet. "Many had lost their boots/But limped on, blood-shod." They are "lame" and "blind," so that while we can see them, they can no longer see. Later, the speaker tells us that "In all my dreams before my helpless sight" he continues to *see* the horrors of a gas attack. "Gas! GAS! Quick, boys!" someone calls, and new senses are introduced as we seem to smell the green, poison gas that chokes the man unable to get his gas mask on in time. As he dies, the speaker hears "the blood/Come gurgling from the froth-corrupted lungs" as the body is tossed into a wagon. Owen uses a simile to try to describe the desperate acts of the man who is gassed: "flound'ring like a man in fire or lime" because he knows his audience, as nonsoldiers, cannot *see* the real event. Finally, after all the images are piled up like the dead bodies in the cart, he concludes his argument:

My friend, you would not tell with such high zest
To children ardent for some desperate glory,
The old lie: *Dulce et decorum est*
Pro Patria mori.

In Randall Jarrell's poem, the "if" isn't even possible. There seems to be no hope, only the inevitable inhumane bureaucratic death by war. The short poem is worth quoting in full:

From my mother's sleep I fell into the State,
And I hunched in its belly till my wet fur froze.
Six miles from earth, loosed from its dream of life,
I woke to black flak and the nightmare fighters.
When I died they washed me out of the turret with a hose.

In Owen's poem, at least we still recognized real men at war; they were men who recognized horror, had nightmares, and felt the loss of their comrades. What is so scary about Jarrell's image is that it conjures up the aloneness of the gunner. He is barely human, no longer a comrade in arms, but a mere animal, a creature no sooner born, his "fur" still "wet," than he is plunged into use by the State as a gunner. If Owen uses irony, so does Jarrell, but it is a colder, harsher irony, as the point of view twists in the last line, and the gunner describes his own end: "When I died they washed me out of the turret with a hose." Thus he speaks not only for himself, but for all those silenced by the bureaucracy and madness of war. Just as Owen's narrator tells the story of his lost comrades, so the narrator here tells a similar tale, but, ironically, it is his story as well as theirs.

The brevity of the poem is like the quick, short life of the young recruit, no sooner born than he is old enough to enlist, and die.

Both poems argue powerfully, through their images and their ironic tone, against war. If the world is still fighting wars it can only mean that politicians just don't read enough poetry.

WRITING THE FIRST DRAFT

Once you have limited the topic, and figured out which strategy is best for the ideas you want to express, you can write the first draft. The first draft is not just an outline. It is an attempt at a full, complete essay, meant to be read by someone else. Write the thesis statement first, as part of the introductory paragraph. Then plan your body paragraphs. A 500-word essay might have a total of five paragraphs, so you'll be writing an introduction (with a thesis), three body paragraphs, and a conclusion. Look closely at the sample essays to see how the writer decided when to start a new paragraph. Look at the use of transitions to start new paragraphs as well. Select the quotes from the works of literature you are using that will support your argument. Each body paragraph should have at least one quotation from the work of literature you are discussing.

Type your draft, double spaced, using the manuscript guidelines for the final copy (94–95). If your instructor allows a handwritten draft, use ink, and double space, leaving wide margins. This will make revision much easier. After you write the first draft, try to get some feedback. Your instructor may read the draft and offer suggestions for revision. In addition, you can exchange drafts with a classmate and offer each other suggestions. Ask the reader if your thesis is clear and whether you have enough quotes to support the thesis.

REVISING

After you receive some suggestions, revise the essay. Think of this as "revision," that is, seeing the essay again. A good revision requires:

rewriting the thesis to make it clearer
checking that there are clear transitions between paragraphs
checking that all quotations are copied correctly
making any necessary corrections for spelling, grammar, and sentence structure

Once you have rethought and rewritten your draft, you are ready to create the final copy of the manuscript. When you submit a manuscript, you must make it look neat and professional. Follow these guidelines:

1. Cover Page

Each essay should have a cover or title page. Center the title of the essay in the middle of the page. About two-thirds down, list:

your full name
your student identification number
the professor's name
the course code number
the assignment number
the date

2. Manuscript Page

All pages are typed and double spaced.
Each page is numbered and headed with your last name in front of the page number.
Leave wide margins: 1 1/2 inch on the left, and 1 inch at the top, bottom, and right-hand side.
Titles of novels, plays, books and any long work of literature (like the epic *Paradise Lost*) must be underlined. Short pieces—poems, short stories— are put in quotation marks each time they are used in the essay, for example, "Filling Station."
If your instructor requires it, be sure you have included a citation with the page on which the quote appears each time you quote from a poem, play, or story in the text. Put the page number in parentheses after the quotation:

Wild Nights–Wild Nights! (264).

If you have any questions about manuscript format, ask your instructor.

RESPONDING TO COMMENTS

When your instructor has read your essay, he/she will return it to you with comments. You should rewrite the essay, using the comments as guidelines for revision. As you plan the revision, pay attention to:

- Basic skills errors: spelling, grammar, sentence structure.
- Use of quotations: did you quote enough/too much?
- Organization: are the paragraphs planned carefully, with clear and effective transitions?
- Thesis: Is the thesis clear, and does the essay support and prove the thesis in the body paragraphs?

After you review the manuscript, you may resubmit it to the instructor. You may also share your revision with classmates to see if the comments have been responded to adequately.

PART TWO

The Elements of Literature

3

Writing about Fiction

Writing about fiction is your chance to enter a house that from the outside looks forbiddingly large and mysterious. But having entered, you find many interesting and delightfully arranged rooms filled with sunlight to explore, all really yours alone to enjoy, examine, and describe.

Although the instructor may review for you formal literary criticism (a large, well-appointed room with great oak beams and stained glass windows), the points to be covered in your writing, and the length of your paper, that paper should reflect your thoughts and feelings about the literary work at hand.

It is important to know, first, that fiction has been described as counterfeiting, a making up and manipulation of a series of events and characters and their thoughts. We first encountered fiction as children when we read or had read to us the classic stories assigned to children from Grimm's *Fairy Tales,* Aesop's *Fables,* and other similar works. Children's fiction, whether classic or contemporary, does not completely help us to understand fiction, but it does indicate how familiar we are with it.

As you write about fiction, you should next ask yourself if you like or dislike the work you read and why. Did you like what happened and the way it happened? In addition, you might consider the possibility that other readers liked the work as much as you did. Why would this be so? What elements of a Chekhov story could be as important to you as to a student in Russia or India or France? Which elements in Shakespeare's plays have made them so universally acclaimed for so many centuries? You may be intrigued by the plot, the events that lead you deeper and deeper into the story. You may share the same emotions as a character, and would do the same thing he or she would do in similar situations. You may have discovered yourself enveloped in a certain mood as you read. Was that an accident?

Great fiction resonates with universal human experience. The rules of human conduct tend to be informally agreed on in many diverse cultures, including primitive ones before there were ten commandments, for example. Earlier peoples had been inclined to behave morally before such conduct became codified by law. The writer often reflects what is already deeply rooted in humankind. It may be these abiding universal truths that make us like a work of fiction.

As you know from the first chapter, there are several schools of literary criticism, some old, some new. Authors, however, rarely write to the beat of such criticism; they are assigned to a particular school after the fact. They may write at a specific time and be influenced by the style and events of that period. However, writers such as Nathaniel Hawthorne, James Joyce, Franz Kafka, Richard Wright, and Flannery O'Connor were innovators of narrative styles, and found ways to write that differed from those of writers who came before them.

Consequently, you'd do well to think of the uniqueness of the writer before you write about the work. When did the author live and where? What was going on at the time that the writer *may* have been influenced by? Where did the writer travel and what happened when she or he got there? What kind of work did the writer do in addition to writing? (Many writers have held a variety of jobs before and while writing; several of them were journalists like Hemingway or physicians like Chekhov.) What books did the writer read? What unusual experiences, if any, did the writer have? Consider that the writer, like those cited above, discovered something new to write about or a new way of writing about something often written before, some aspect of characterization or narrative that illustrates an unusual perception of the human condition. ·

Remember that the blank page for the writer is like a new world about to be discovered—just as it is for you. You and the writer are heirs to the oldest means of communication exclusive of voice sounds and hand signs. (The telephone is only 115 years old; television is barely 50.) In the life of humankind writing itself is a relatively recent means of making communications visible—perhaps something over 7500 years old. And at the very start of this literary history there was fiction. The Egyptian *Tales of the Magicians,* a collection of stories from about 4000 B.C., naturally supposes even earlier beginnings. Other narrative works have come from India, ancient Israel, the kingdoms of the Euphrates, the Greeks, the Arabs, and from many other peoples and places.

The creative urge to tell stories is universally one of the strongest emotions in human beings. Fiction, of course, is not all pure creation; sometimes it is the reworking of experience or communal history—that is, making reality fit fictional needs which then often go beyond reality to make specific points. Our earliest fiction consisted of moral writing; good things happened to good people (or animals) and bad things happened to bad people (or animals). Perhaps this is as it should be, but it is not what most of us understand about reality today. The drive to write fiction that in part or whole is didactic (morally instructive) is still obvious in the work of many contemporary writers of fiction.

Writing about fiction should be something of both challenge and opportunity, exploration and discovery. What does *this* writer have to say—and how does he or she say it? you might ask yourself. A story or a novel is a special room in the house you are visiting. Unlike television where you see the story, fiction makes you envision it, stretch your knowledge and imagination to match the author's. Understand, though, that most writers *are* writers because writing is for them the most lasting, perhaps even the most natural way they can reach out to others. "Writing," of course, is a combination of thinking *and* writing, as we shall see.

THE ELEMENTS OF FICTION

Once you sense the uniqueness of an author and the significance of his or her work, you should be able to write critically about it. Critical writing requires you to deal with key elements of fiction. These elements are discussed in the section that follows.

Plot

Plot is the arrangement of related events, however simple or complex, in the narrative of a work of fiction with the result that subsequently some conflict around which the story revolves will be concluded. (All fiction does not contain the same degree of conflict, and there is fiction in which there is very little conflict.) Plotting a story is the ordering of a world and the lives of the characters who inhabit it. William Faulkner wrote: "I like to think of the world I created as being a kind of keystone in the universe; that small as the keystone is, if it were ever taken away the universe itself would collapse."

Real life, however, is rarely within our ability to control. If we could, "splendid economy" is what such ordering could be called, instead of Henry James' observation that life is splendid waste, "all is conclusion and confusion."

Aristotle in his *Poetics* calls plot the first element of drama or epic, which is composed of three elements: 1) a beginning that presumes additional action, 2) a middle that considers previous action and presumes succeeding action, and 3) an end that requires attention to earlier events but anticipates no further action.

Over the years Aristotle's three elements have been increased to five, more clearly-defined fundamentals of plot. They are: 1) the beginning and exposition which set the plot (or plots) in motion; 2) rising action, a series of actions, each of which causes another to begin and which considers the importance of tension and conflict (earlier critics used "conflict" and "crisis" interchangeably); 3) the climax, the most critical section of the narrative; 4) falling action, a lessening of tension, during which time some degree of tension (or suspension) is still maintained together with the explanation of the related events, sometimes called the denouement; 5) the resolution of the conflict—the happy or unhappy ending.

Whether you prefer the pure Aristotelian formula for plot or its expanded contemporary version, remember that plot in fiction is the structuring or ordering of the narrative. How does Kate Chopin plot a story in a brief moment of time, while Kafka seems to embrace all of time in a story like "A Hunger Artist"? How does Hernando Tellez create and heighten conflict in "Just Lather, That's

All,'' and how is it resolved? Why does Leslie Marmon Silko divide ''The Man
to Send Rain Clouds'' into sections? And does Arna Bontemps' ''A Summer
Tragedy'' conform to Aristotle's definition of plot? These are some of the questions you might want to consider as you write about fiction. (Plot is in the map
room of the house.)

Character

The people you come to know in stories or novels are characters; they create
action in the narrative. They tend to be the focus of the work. John Dryden
believed that ''the story is the least part'' of a work, the character the most
important. The writer creates the characters and supplies us with the information
that allows us to identify, positively or negatively, with them. We know something
about how the characters look, live, and think; often we know about their jobs
and their social status, their aspirations and problems. We enter their heads—as
we cannot with real people in real life—and share their emotions; we have access
to the most secret and intimate corridors of their being. It is here where character
motivation originates and plot commences. If the writer has done well, the character is revealed to the reader, act by act, spoken word by spoken word, thought
by thought, like a flower unfolding petal by petal in the summer sun.

Not infrequently you will find characters so strongly drawn that they
become the titles of the works they are in, for example, Charles Dickens'
Martin Chuzzlewit, or Henry James' *Daisy Miller,* or Herman Melville's *Billy
Budd, Foretopman,* or Stephen Crane's *Maggie: A Girl of the Streets.* Short
stories like Hawthorne's ''Young Goodman Brown'' and Gloria Naylor's ''Kiswana Browne'' indicate the continuing popularity of character titles involving
people of all kinds of stations who function as fictional heroes and heroines.

Good characters must have dimension—that is, not merely inhabit the
narrative for the sake of being there. The character must function; plot must turn
on the character's actions; dialogue between characters must move plot as well
as enlarge the character. It is crucial that we know everything about a character
that is pertinent to the story, and perhaps that knowledge will resonate beyond
the bounds of fiction. For example, we *want* to know what happens to the hero
and heroine in ''The Lady with the Pet Dog,'' for we invest in them as people
and wonder about their destinies. That is what good writing and vivid characterization do. (Character can be found in the screening room.)

Point of View

Point of view is the position in which the writer places the character, around
whom move all the elements of fiction. Point of view, like the defined area seen
through a camera lens, is the frame or boundary of a work of fiction. Frequently
it is through the point of view that we discover different ways of telling a story.

Traditionally there are three basic points of view: the first person or ''I'';

the somewhat experimental second person or "you"; and the third person "he," "she," "it," or "they."

First-person point of view is the method by which the author centrally positions one person through whom the story is told. Every detail of the work is filtered through that character who cannot intimately know others; he or she is the "I" character of the first-person singular. This is a limiting, but often effective way of writing, but that may be precisely what the author desires. This might be called a high-intensity point of view, providing the author with a special and perhaps unique voice in a strictly circumscribed world. Joyce's "Araby" and Louise Erdrich's "Snares" are two examples of the use of the internal or "I" voice.

Daniel Defoe's *Robinson Crusoe,* Joseph Conrad's *Lord Jim,* and Herman Melville's *Moby Dick* are but three of many novels in which writers have used the first-person voice effectively. The first-person point of view dictates that the protagonist can examine himself inside out, but most constantly decipher the acts and words of others to examine himself.

(Untraditionally, however, there can be more than one "I" character in the same work. For example, if there are three people at the scene of a crime—the perpetrator, the victim, and a witness—the crime can be related by each character in turn, therefore bringing different first-person points of view to the story.)

The use of the third-person or external voice gives writers far more lee-way—though they may not use it. The "I" becomes "he" or "she" and this lets the writer use the *limited* or *pseudo* third person, focusing not on several characters, but one, as in Wright's "The Man Who Was Almost a Man." From this point of view, the writer moves that character from a distance, and does not become one with the "I." No other character is really penetrated, or certainly not to the degree the protagonist has been. Sometimes, as in Bontemps' "A Summer Tragedy," two characters, Jennie and Jeff Patton, can become the third person of a story. Third person can be compared to a camera that has been focused between closeup and wide-angle, and it is this point of view many authors use to make us see a resemblance between fiction and the real world. The interior experiences of a singular major character are such that we can readily share them. Nothing stands between the writer and reader but the manipulated distance provided by the third person. Gone is the intrusive authorial voice of past use of the point of view (often opinionated, or editorializing and addressing the reader directly by the pronoun "you"). In modern fiction the characters speak; no authors are allowed.

Readers tend to identify more readily with one major character, though they seem to prefer the larger reality offered by the third-person voice over the first-person. Both, however, are widely used in the short story.

Unlimited third-person and omniscient or objective points of view are essentially the same. Herein, the author views all characters from an equal, objective stance; she can enter all their minds or none; the writer can share knowledge of one or more characters with every other character in the work.

With the omniscient or unlimited third person and a large number of characters, through the use of the *interior monologue,* much like the dramatic soliloquy, the author can let us know how much one character knows about another. This achieves dynamic progress in the same way film is used to create anticipation and tension through montage. But sacrificed by this point of view is the sense of closeness to character found in the first person or limited third person. Here the author is truly a god, aiming characters at each other, constructing plots, establishing settings, issuing subjects and themes couched in a variety of styles, all conveyed through a team of characters.

Leo Tolstoy's *War and Peace* is a great model for the use of the omniscient point of view. The novel is a vibrant animism that conveys the movements of people and history. Tolstoy uses more than 500 characters ranging from peasant to Napoleon, with the key players meeting or crossing paths at crucial times after earlier being introduced in alternating chapters. The distance between author and characters is not always equal, since the major actors are only three of the multitude: Natasha Rostova, Prince Andrei Bolkonski, and Pierre Bezukhov.

Shifts in point of view may be indicated by a new paragraph, a space break in the narrative, or nothing at all. E.M. Forster declared that with an effective shift of viewpoint the writer has the power "to bounce the reader into accepting what he says." Dickens' *Bleak House,* Stevenson's *Dr. Jekyll and Mr. Hyde,* as well as Tolstoy's epic, present examples of shifting points of view. Shifting points of view may come as relief to some readers, a change of pace. For the writer, they expand or contract perception, allow a closeup or telephoto angle.

Tense usage combined with point of view offers tempting avenues for experimentation. Present tense makes narrative seem as though events are occurring as you read them; past tense is more leisurely and is used with greater frequency. A writer might shift point of view between first person, third person, and omniscient for certain specific effects (closeness or distance) and at the same time shift from past to present tense for certain other effects, for instance, pacing—speeding or slowing down the action. Traditionally, however, fiction is usually presented in only one tense and one point of view.

Setting

Setting is the physical place where action may occur in a narrative. That place is of immense importance in establishing the mood of a work of fiction.

Just as characters often are the titles of novels and stories they are in, such as Jamaica Kincaid's "Girl," Kay Boyle's "Astronomer's Wife," and Bharati Mukerjee's "Hindus," places, too, are frequently titles: Langston Hughes' "On the Road," Eudora Welty's "A Worn Path," and Ernest Hemingway's "A Clean, Well-lighted Place," all found in your authology.

We feel a sense of comfort with the familiar. When we read a book whose settings are known to us, or see a film set in a city that we either live in or have visited, we feel closer to the story. Yet, we are curious about places we know little about. Ray Bradbury's "August 2026: There Will Come Soft Rains" intrigues us because the setting is in a time none of us can envision with assurance. Edgar Allan Poe's "The Masque of the Red Death," considered one of his greatest stories, has a setting that is as much in Prince Prospero's mind as it is in the castle to which he retires to escape the plague. We are drawn into the story to ricochet between the "real" and another level of imagination, terror.

As we know, a setting in fiction is not fixed as in many plays—is not real, but a construction of words designed to give the reader a sense of place through description. But settings can also be deceptive. Shirley Jackson's "The Lottery" begins in a small American town (like the one in "Young Goodman Brown" quite possibly) on a day that is "clear and sunny," but ends with a character screaming, "It isn't fair, it isn't right." (Jackson, like Poe, is a masterful writer of Gothic horror.)

Settings can be physical as well as symbolic, as Nadine Gordimer's "The Train from Rhodesia" and Welty's title suggest. In short, setting is where the fiction lives.

Tone

Tone, which we also find in poetry and drama, is the "attitude" of the author in a work of fiction. When we speak of a story as being happy or sad, comic or tragic, ironic or satiric, we are trying to establish the writer's attitude toward his or her materials. Sometimes it is easy to establish the tone of a story. For example, the very title of Arna Bontemps' "A Summer Tragedy" indicates the author's perspective on the action. At other times, we have a sudden shift in tone that turns the title into an ironic commentary, as in the conclusion of Hernando Tellez's "Just Lather, That's All." Tone can also be a complex subject, embracing matters of setting and mood, characterization, narrative action, and style. Consider Amy Tan's story "Two Kinds." The story presents a young, somewhat rebellious girl who knows she doesn't have the talents her mother ascribes to her. Yet, there are moments when, briefly, she thinks she does. Then comes the moment when she deliberately—though this might not altogether be the case—performs badly enough to make her mother have doubts. As behavior shifts, the tone also shifts from small hope to failure and to guilt because Jing-mei has failed to keep alive the immigrant's dream of becoming "anything you wanted to be in America." The "voice" changes, becomes more reflective and mellow when Jing-mei reaches thirty and looks back on her childhood. Moreover, there is another voice in the story, the mother's, which lends tension to the story, heightens the conflict between mother and daughter and between reality and possibility. Here the tone is at first hopeful, then desperate, and finally, defeated. The reconciliation when Jing-mei is an adult is sad and touching, and this is the final tonality in an admittedly complex tale.

Symbolism

A symbol is a representation of a reality on one level that has a corresponding reality on another level; symbols are things that represent other things by habit, association, or convention. Symbols in fiction, poetry, and drama possess specific points of reference created by the writer to lead you to and inside the work. *Symbols* are most often associated with *allegory* (Greek: "to speak other"). Allegory has two levels of meaning, but the second meaning is to be read beneath and concurrent with the surface story and may well itself be an extended story. In Kay Boyle's "The Astronomer's Wife," symbolism and allegory are relatively easy to discern. You may wish to discuss the symbolism expressed by the occupations of Mrs. Ames' husband and the plumber, or the allegory that further describes *where* they work, or the similarities between a plumbers' pipe and an astronomer's telescope. In Franz Kafka's "A Hunger Artist," a more complex story, you can find several meanings that can be read as ironic or tragic, as well as allegorical. Edgar Allan Poe's "The Masque of the Red Death" abounds in allegory. A critical reading of these works should help you understand the various levels of meaning they contain.

Style

Style is found in the way a work of fiction is written. George Henry Lewes, who lived with Marian Evans (pen name: George Eliot), listed five rules of style: 1) economy (conciseness with precision); 2) simplicity; 3) sequential development of plot; 4) the inevitability of climax; and 5) variety.

These rules seem to still be valid even though language has changed tremendously since Lewes' time. But modern applications also see style as the way certain rhythms are employed in fiction writing; the way authors choose their words and use abstract, concrete, and figurative language; and the way they handle all the traditional elements of fiction—plot, character, point of view, setting, and theme. These, too, have been modified by time, and as these have been altered, so too has the heading under which more recent works fall: post-modernism.

But for many writers style is simply the way they write, the way words occur to them while shaping their fiction. For others, style may have developed over time through studying, consciously or subconsciously, the work of still other writers.

Writers who have journalism backgrounds, like Hemingway or Martha Gellhorn, may write in a style quite different from the one used by writers who also write or have written poetry, like Robert Penn Warren. Few poets, Walt Whitman being one of the exceptions, emerge from a background in journalism. There are many factors that may help to shape a style. And of course there are writers without any writing background who love language and ultimately find themselves to be writers.

Hemingway, whose style a generation of writers tried to copy, is known for his Spartan prose which is almost devoid of adjectives and adverbs, and for his use of plain language. These helped to make him clearly understandable and accessible. Ford Madox Ford said "Hemingway's words strike you, each one, as if they were pebbles fetched from a brook."

William Faulkner's style is rotund, full-blown, expansive, and not very accessible—which led Hemingway to say of him, "Poor Faulkner. Does he really think big emotions come from big words?"

But then critic Max Eastman said Hemingway had "a literary style . . . of wearing false hair on the chest." Both Faulkner and Hemingway are Nobel laureates in literature.

Theme

To some readers theme and subject mean the same thing. They are quite different. Matthew Arnold wrote that "All depends on subject: choose a fitting action, penetrate yourself with the feeling of its situations; this done, everything will follow."

Theme, however, really is the distillation of subject; it makes relevant all the words that are used to frame the theme, which is the fine print of subject. The following brief dialogue examines the difference between subject and theme.

STUDENT A: "What's the book about?"
STUDENT B: "War." [Subject]
STUDENT A: "War?"
STUDENT B: "Actually, the horrors experienced by soldiers at the Battle of the Bulge. [Theme]

The subject is general; the theme is a specific statement about the subject. The same principle might be applied to Tolstoy, who wrote about *armies* in *War and Peace,* and Hemingway, whose writings included pieces on the *units* of armies in three wars. The poet Wilfred Owen once said "My subject is War, and the pity of War. The poetry is in the pity." Owen thus defines the difference between subject and theme in his own work.

INTERPRETING FICTION

Your interpretation of a literary work begins with accepting its theme, its diction and construction, what the work conveys to you, and your reaction to it. You accept the writing as a complete entity, a work of art, that possesses values you and other readers respect.

That done, you will find it worthwhile to review the elements of fiction to see if they are present or mostly present in the story you are interpreting. Then it may be expedient to note the theme of the story. If we took Chekhov's "The Lady with the Pet Dog," would we be seeing another "star-crossed lovers" theme or quite some other theme?

You might try to describe the kind of man Gurov is and decide whether or not there is irony in how he has changed by the end of the story. How has his openness to the "encounters of life" contributed to the plot? How effective are plot and character in support of theme? Point of view? With the questions and your answers digested, you can then move to the author's motive, if any, for writing the story. Chekhov is very good at detail that is important to his stories, so it will help if you read this (or any other story) more than once.

There are not, really, as many kinds of fiction as there are poetry, but it would be unfair to poetry to say that it does not require as much analysis as fiction; the amount of analysis depends on the work under study, not because it is one genre or the other. Most stories, however, are longer than most poems, and will require longer, more analytical reading. Some poems provide clues to their meanings by the way they are structured on the page, with some lines indented, very brief stanzas, or the use of punctuation: colons, for instance, or dashes. In a poem, these clues tend to leap out.

Such is not the case with most fiction. Outward appearances on the printed page reveal nothing. Reading is the only way to dig out the elements necessary for you to write about fiction. A first reading of a story may reveal its plot and then its theme. Plots generally come to life first, but not the theme within, so it may take a second or third reading before theme emerges. Plot, as you know, is the element in fiction where tension and conflict are found.

Once you have a good idea of what the story is about you can gather the characters on stage to see how well they have carried and moved plot, if their motivations, inner thoughts, dialogues and actions support your possible conclusions about the theme. You will want to describe the function of each character as part of your analysis.

Anton Chekhov said, "Cut a good story anywhere and it will bleed." (He was a doctor.) Would the story you're reading lose anything if it had not been written the way it is? Could you cross out a paragraph and still have the story make sense, or eliminate a character without disturbing the plot? Imagine Philip Roth's "The Conversion of the Jews" without the janitor, Yakov Blotnik; would the story still work? Is the protagonist, Ozzie Freedman, unreasonable? Can you find, subtly located, the reason for Ozzie's behavior, which explains the nature of the conflict? Crucial differences between Itzie and Ozzie arise early in the story. How do they become manifest at the climax of the story?

Notice the shifts in points of view. Do they help you to understand the story, and in which ways? How do the breaks in the story add to its tension? These are the kinds of questions you should ask yourself and find answers to in order to write cogently about any story.

Remember that interpretations of fiction are not engraved in stone. Unless an author tells us of her intention in writing the story, or what the theme most assuredly is, or why a character does this or says that, we simply cannot know for sure why a story is the way it is. We just examine what has been given to us and come to the best interpretation we can which is, as it can only be, your opinion.

EVALUATING FICTION

A famous painter said "A painting is valuable to you if *you* like it." In the same light, a work of fiction is valuable to you if you appreciate it for what it is. But that is only the beginning. Almost none of us is comfortable being alone in an evaluative process.

Students of literature can take heart: There is a proven track record of great fiction, whether we agree with it or not. In any case, the record is always changing. Herman Melville may be on the record for a number of years, and then he is off it; the same with Henry James and Virginia Woolf. The record may showcase at a given time some of the great Russian writers—Dostoyevski, Chekhov, and Tolstoy, for example—but never cite Leonid Andreyev. Some astoundingly good writers have never been on the record, like Martha Gellhorn. It would be a serious mistake not to read the record for information and assistance.

Great fiction engages the universe and millions of readers, each of whom relates to it differently, yet somehow the same. And that is the way we really are. Great fiction has the ability to draw us into it as individuals and as members of a community called humanity stuck in space. We can find knowledge and comfort in fiction, pride and sorrow. Fiction is, after all, merely a reflection of what we are, have been, and perhaps may be.

4

Writing about Poetry

Poetry is generally acknowledged to be the oldest form of literature, but the "problem of defining it is the problem of defining its extraordinariness," wrote one critic.

The earliest poetry we know is narrative poetry, which reflected the history, celebrations, beliefs, and mores of ancient peoples in the Egyptian offering lists, utterances, and papyri; in the Greek epics, the Indian Vedas, the Norse sagas, the Hebrew Old Testament, the Babylonian Gilgamesh epic, and elsewhere. Robert Graves called these narratives a "dramatic shorthand record." Cicero believed that the poet performed invaluable service by recording the deeds of national heroes and noble men. What poetry *is* and what it *does* are questions that have been debated for centuries.

Matthew Arnold said, "There are two offices of poetry—one to add to one's store of thoughts and feelings—another to compose and elevate the mind by sustained tone, numerous allusions, and a grand style." Arnold's is a late definition of poetry which for centuries had been considered a kind of *fiction,* wherein stories were told and a "faigning" (feigning) observable. Sir Philip Sidney thought poetry was "distinctive" because it joined philosophy and history, a theory that John Donne also believed. William Wordsworth in his *Preface* saw the debate about what poetry is as one concerned with the differences between "matter of fact and science." He was joined in this opinion by Samuel Taylor Coleridge and Leigh Hunt. There is for all discussion, however, one monumental difference today between poetry and prose, and it is that prose mimics ordinary speech, while poetic language is extraordinary in the selection of words it uses and in its metrical rhythms. A stanza from Donne's sardonic "Song" (Go and Catch and Falling Star) provides an example of unusual language filled with bite and imagery:

> Go and catch a falling star
>   Get with child a mandrake root,
> Tell me where all past years age,
>   Or who cleft the Devil's foot,

Teach me to hear mermaids singing,
Or to keep off envy's stinging,
    And find
    What wind
Serves to advance an honest mind.

In this single stanza we find stated divisions between "matter of fact" and science, and myth and personal observation. (Donne, after a rakish youth, became a clergyman.) Prose, it was believed by the leading Romantic writers, was better suited for scientific exposition than poetry. Thomas Mann insisted that it was "a fruitless and futile mania" for critics to keep probing for differences between the works of prose writers and poets. Ezra Pound agreed, saying that "all essays about 'poetry' are usually not only dull but inaccurate" and without value.

Poetry is further distinguished by structure or form and its use of meter, which produces rhythm and rhyme. Conversely, some poetry relies heavily on imagery and very little on rhythm and rhyme. In sum, the now traditional differences between poetry and prose are these: poetry *may* be written in meter, but prose is not; poetry *may* use rhyme, while prose does not; poetry most often uses "a special language," but, for the most part, prose does not. (Joyce, of course, would be one of several exceptions.)

The major characteristic of poetry as it evolved through the ages has become its ability to distill monumental themes down to their essences. (We rarely today see a poem that fills a book, like *The Iliad* or *The Odyssey*.) In a time when Americans are said to be angry about and alienated from government, the following two poems might be considered not only prophetic, but good examples of the distillation of themes that have always concerned us. The first, "America" by Claude McKay, is in traditional, fourteen-line, iambic pentameter, sonnet form. The second, by e.e. cummings, "next to of course god," is in "open" or "free verse" form. Consider not only the topic, but the differences in structure, language, and tone:

Although she feeds me bread of bitterness,
And sinks into my throat her tiger's tooth,
Stealing my breath of life, I will confess
I love this cultured hell that tests my youth!
Her vigor flows like tides into my blood,
Giving me strength against her hate.
Her bigness sweeps my being like a flood.
Yet as a rebel fronts a kind in state,
I stand within her walls with not a shred
Of terror, malice, not a word of jeer.
Darkly I gaze into the days ahead,
And see her might and granite wonders there,
Beneath the touch of Time's unerring hand,
Like priceless treasures sinking in the sand.

• • •

"next to of course god america i
love you land of the pilgrims; and so forth oh
say can you see by the dawn's early my
country 'tis of centuries come and go
and are no more what of it we should worry
in every language even deafanddumb
thy sons acclaim your glorious name by gorry
by jingo by gee by gosh by gum
why talk of beauty what could be more beautiful
than these heroic happy dead
who rushed like lions to the roaring slaughter
they did not stop to think they died instead
then shall the voice of liberty be mute."

He spoke. And drank rapidly a glass of water.

A single reading of a poem, short or long, is not enough to perceive its meaning, for a poem is somewhat like a mystery to be solved, or a language to be understood. Poetry should be studied line by line. Because of its nature to compress or distill, every word in a poem tends to bear more weight than every word in a story or novel. "Sound out" a poem; read it aloud to detect what silent readings may not offer up. Better still, go to poetry readings remembering that poems were originally *sung* and that there are still places in the world where poets and sometimes musical instruments are called singers.

It is important to know when, approximately, a poem was written; as suggested in the fiction section, it is also helpful to know something about the author and his or her life. A poem's title may also give you a clue as to its theme, and with each reading you'll discover more about the work and find yourself responding to it. That's what the poet wants; that's what any writer wants, because the crucial importance about a poem is that you, the reader, come to feel what the poet wants you to. If this occurs, that means you have penetrated his or her imaginative arena, unlocked the mystery, understood the language.

Poets, being "the athletes of language," according to Robert Boynton, are forever challenging our ability to keep up with them. They are like drummers in the band called Literature: they set the pace, diminish or augment it with new or different chords, "sound," images, signals. If we as players somehow lose the beat, we need only "listen" closely to the drummer to get back to it. Poetry is not confined to books; folk singers, blues singers, rockers, and rappers are "the poets of everyday," their lyrics perhaps more current, but certainly linked to the way many people have thought and felt over time.

Your understanding of and sensitivities about popular music may help you with the study of poetry and strengthen the confidence you have in your ability to understand, enjoy, and write about poetry. Like fiction, poetry tells us stories, but they are stories in miniature. The poet leaves it to you to open the work and see his or her world in which you, too, live.

THE ELEMENTS OF POETRY

When you have come to feel the importance of a poet and the special qualities of his or her work, you have reached the stage where you should be capable of writing critical essays about that work. However, critical writing requires that you deal with the major elements of poetry, which are detailed in the following section.

Types of Poetry

Broadly and structurally speaking there are two basic kinds of poetry. The first and by far the more traditional, is the "closed" form, which follows a pattern that we may find in a sonnet or villanelle, "heroic" or "blank" verse (*verso sciolto*). Closed poetry abides by rules of form set down long ago and rarely departs from them. These rules determine the length of each line, and where rhyme and accent are placed. Of course, as poetry evolved, various authors experimented with the traditional forms.

The "open" form, often called "free verse" or *vers libre,* is considered to be an American-created form as opposed to the closed forms, which are European. The open form relies heavily not on rhyme and not necessarily on the traditional metric feet that create rhythm, but on a perhaps more subtle rhythm called "cadence," and imagery.

Beneath the headings of closed and open are many types of poetry, easily a dozen or even more, which are variations of three major styles in poetry: narrative (treated earlier in this chapter), dramatic monologue, and lyric. Matthew Arnold characterized the monologue as being "The dialogue of the mind with itself." Believed to be popular only since the Middle Ages, it nevertheless is rooted much deeper in the poetic imagination, back to the epics and sagas and papyri, to the Greek plays, which are written in poetry. Everyone knows the beginning of Hamlet's soliloquy (or monologue)—"To be or not to be," spoken while Hamlet ponders revenge. The critical situations of characters in all literature have always been the ideal times for them to range about within themselves for solutions. In the following example of dramatic monologue, Alfred, Lord Tennyson places "Ulysses" in a very special place located between the allegorical renderings of Dante and the myths related by the Homerian *Iliad* and *Odyssey.* In this section, Ulysses from afar contemplates the virtues and perhaps defects in his son:

> This is my son, mine own Telemachus,
> To whom I leave the sceptre and the isle—
> Well-loved of me, discerning to fulfil
> This labour, by slow prudence to make mild
> A rugged people, and thro' soft degrees
> Subdue them to the useful and the good.
> Most blameless is he, centered in the sphere

Of common duties, decent not to fail
In offices of tenderness, and pay
Meet adoration to my household gods,
When I am gone. He works his work, I mine.

"Ulysses" is in blank verse—metered in iambic pentameter without rhyme. It is a closed poem.

Lyric poetry is distinguished by the personal posture of the poet—how he or she views the world. The language is strong yet plain and striking. We are made aware of the world around us through the personification of the elements of which it is composed. Yet lyric poetry is controlled through its structure which defines it, too, as closed, as we see in Wordsworth's "Composed Upon Westminster Bridge, September 3, 1802":

Earth has not anything to show more fair:
Dull would be he of soul who could pass by
A sight so touching in its majesty:
This city doth, like a garment, wear
The beauty of the morning; silent, bare,
Ships, towers, domes, theatres, and temples lie
Open unto the fields, and to the sky;
All bright and glittering in the smokeless air.
Never did the sun more beautifully steep
In his first splendour, valley, rock, or hill;
Ne'er saw I, never felt, a calm so deep!
The river glideth at his own sweet will:
Dear God! the very houses seem asleep;
And all that mighty heart is lying still!

William Wordsworth became the standard-bearer of lyric poetry (lyric: "fit to be sung with a lyre or harp"), with his 1798 publication of *Lyrical Ballads* (first edition; there were three). By contrast, in the United States Walt Whitman "said his 'God be with you' to the European poets and then parted company with them irrevocably . . . and with his American colleagues, too. He sang no sweet songs, but long, loosely metered chants," wrote critic Max Herzberg. *Leaves of Grass* was Whitman's mark upon the land and mind of America in 1855, and, shortly after, the world.

An example of Whitman's innovative open poetry is his "Cavalry Crossing a Ford," set during the Civil War:

A line in long array where they wind betwixt green islands,
They take a serpentine course, their arms flash in the sun—hark to the musical
    clank,
Behold the silvery river, in it the splashing horses loitering stop to drink,
Behold the brown-faced men, each group, each person a picture, the negligent rest
    on the saddles,
Some emerge on the opposite bank, others are just entering the ford—while,
Scarlet and blue and snowy white,
The guidon flags flutter gayly in the wind.

"Calvary Crossing a Ford" contains very long lines and some short lines. Basically, the language is not used to yield thundering interior or metric rhythms. Like a serpent ("serpentine course"), the cavalry winds from one bank of the river to the other. The emphasis is on alliteration, the repetition of consonant or vowel sounds at the beginning of words: "A line in long array"; "emerge . . . opposite . . . others . . . entering . . . flags flutter . . . .'"; "Scarlet and blue and snowy white" not only is alliterative, but has a subtle rhythm as well. The intent of this open poem is to create a picture through word images, and a single picture usually captures one event in progress, "narrates" one story that opens on a wider world. In this case that world is the Civil War.

Voice and Tone

Got an attitude? So does a poem, because the poet put it there. Tone is the voice we hear and it is this that conveys the attitude. Tone tells us the way the poet feels about you, himself or herself, the world. Gwendolyn Brooks' diction in "The Bean Eaters" is designed to make us feel a very particular way:

> They eat beans mostly, this old yellow pair.
> Dinner is a casual affair.
> Plain chipware on a plain and creaking wood,
> Tin flatware.
>
> Two who are Mostly Good.
> Two have lived their day,
> But keep on putting on their clothes
> And putting things away.
>
> And remembering . . .
> Remembering, with twinklings and twinges,
> As they lean over the beans in their rented back room that
>   is full of beads and receipts and dolls and cloths,
> Tobacco crumbs, vases and fringes.

Describe the tone of "The Bean Eaters." Note the several images that describe the condition of these elderly people, and the empathy Brooks expresses. In some ways there is a similarity between the determination of the couple to "keep on" doing things and Ulysses' pledge "to strive, to seek, to find and not to yield" (in the final stanza). In Brooks' poem, also note the structure with both short and long lines, and rhyme, though it is irregular. Is the poem open, closed, or a combination of both?

Note the differences in tone—attitude—and structure between Brooks' poem and Cyn. Zarco's poem:

> Asparagus
>
> There's a washcloth
> with a picture of asparagus
> in my bathroom.

56

Did you know
that Filipinos were picked
to grow asparagus in the West
because they were short
and built close to the ground?

I'm 5′3″. I don't use
that washcloth anymore.

There is a cleanness and brevity of line in this poem that contains a tone of defiance about the past—and the future. It is an open, lyrical poem, but you have to fill in some of the story.

Sound is frequently associated with voice and tone. But the creation of sound in a poem, that is, making you seem to hear sound, is a process of diction. Poets select certain words that we have come to associate with certain sounds. "Splash," "buzz," and "hiss," for example, are commonly associated with water, flying insects, geese, and serpents. The Greek word, onomatopoeia, simply means naming a thing or action by imitating it vocally. Sound often may be sensed in the way a poem is written, for example in Coleridge's "Kubla Khan," before we are actually aware of the sound. But do remember that most poets think about sound because their work traditionally was heard, not read, although there is much poetry written today primarily to be read. The utilization of rhythm, meter, alliteration, assonance, and dissonance (see the glossary in your anthology) are crucial in producing sound in a poem.

Imagery and Symbolism

Poetry would not be poetry without imagery, which we find, along with symbolism, even in the earliest works. Homer gives us the "Rosy-fingered dawn" and the "wine-dark sea," images that have lingered more than 2000 years. An image may be created with one or several related words used to make us feel that we are "living in a poem" through hearing, feeling, tasting, seeing, or smelling. The symbolist movement began in France late in the nineteenth century. Its members believed poetry could better express and explore the human psyche by recreating human consciousness through symbols, which often reflect inexpressible emotions. In the U.S., the "imagists" were the American counterparts of the symbolists.

Sometimes the major image in a poem is indicated by its title, as in imagist Amy Lowell's "Taxi":

When I go away from you
The world beats dead
Like a slackened drum.
I call out for you against the jutted stars
And shout into the ridges of the wind.
Streets coming fast,

One after the other,
Wedge you away from me.
And the lamps of the city prick my eyes
So that I can no longer see your face.
Why should I leave you,
To wound myself upon the sharp edges of the night?

All the related images employed here define a situation. What is it, what's going on? How does the text of the poem fracture the ''I'' and ''you'' found in five of the twelve lines? Is this an open or closed poem?

In poetry (and fiction) the function of symbolism is to stand for a state of mind instead of representing a specific object. For example, in everyday life, we know that the green light tells us that we may walk across the street, while the red one advises us not to. The red, white, and blue flag with thirteen stripes and fifty stars is a symbol having many meanings to Americans. If the flag were green with black stripes and red stars it would have very little meaning for most of us because, as Kenneth Burke wrote, ''A symbol is the verbal parallel to a pattern of experience,'' and our experiences have prepared us not for green, black, and red, but red, white, and blue, the flag that stands for the United States of America.

Some poets take standard symbols and create new ones that have reference to the old, familiar ones. For it is in the nature of poetry to create newer and possibly more accurate symbols for the world we know. The first and final stanzas of Gerald Vizenor's ''Haiku'' offer us familiar symbols with uncommon meanings:

october sunflowers
like rows of defeated soldiers
leaning in the frost

october wind
garage doors open and close
wings of the moth

Although the term ''image'' calls up something we have seen, in poetic terms we are considering specific, related words that have to do with sensual (the five senses) experiences.

A symbol, on the other hand, stands for something other than what it is.

Simile and Metaphor

These terms are often considered to be similar; but a simile compares two objects of different categories, while a metaphor substitutes one object for another.

''Johnson is as tall as Bird'' is *not* a simile, but ''Johnson is as tall as a small tree'' is, because of the dissimilarity of the references or comparisons. Similes use ''like'' or ''as''—''He ran like the wind.'' Metaphors also substitute one thing for another, hence ''tree'' for ''Bird.'' Aristotle believed that the ability to find resemblance in disparate things was ''the best gift of the poet.''

In Maya Angelou's "To a Husband" we find powerful metaphors in the opening lines:

Your voice at times a fist
    Tight in your throat
Jabs ceaselessly at phantoms
    In the room,
Your hand a carved and
    Skimming boat
Goes down the Nile
    To point out Pharaoh's tomb.

Note the absence of "like" in the first and fifth lines of the stanza.

    Analogy is often associated with simile and metaphor. It presumes a resemblance between two things. This example is from Francis Bacon: "*Money* is like *muck,* not good unless it's spread." *Allusion,* also to be found in this company, is an indirect reference to some person, place, object, or event within a literary work. Babette Deutsch's poem, "Disasters of War: Goya at the Museum," alludes to a famous painting by Francisco y Lucientes Goya (1746–1828) that hangs in the Prado Museum in Madrid.

Diction and Syntax

Diction is the conscious manipulation of language. It has been described as the clothes words wear. But, since words wear out with use and become cliché, for permanence as well as poetic sensibility, diction should suggest rather than state. And the use of symbolism, metaphor, and simile, which in themselves require linguistic knowledge and dexterity, can only be effective through judicious diction—the selection and use of poetic language.

    Syntax is the way words are organized in order to have meaning; words so formed become sentences and phrases, which in turn can become poems, stories, novels, or plays, or today's big newspaper story. The word selection or diction in Octavio Paz's "Engaged" is supported by a syntax that seems deceptively repetitious:

Stretching out on the grass
a boy and a girl.
Sucking their oranges, giving kisses
like waves exchanging foam.

Stretched out on the beach
a boy and a girl.
Sucking their limes, giving their kisses.
like clouds exchanging foam.

Stretched out underground
a boy and a girl.
Saying nothing, never kissing,
giving silence for silence.

The poet has described, with slight differences, places where there are always "stretched out" "a boy and a girl," who are "giving" their kisses until the final stanza. Then the first and last two lines surprise. We want to say at the end, "Wait a minute," and reread the poem to absorb that final difference, not so much in the syntax, which led us there, as much as the *place* that makes the disruption in behavior, tone, and meaning. Note the similes within the syntax.

Meter and Rhythm

In Greek, meter means *metron* or measure. Most consistently used in closed poetry (which need not necessarily be "traditional"), meter is the regular recurrence of a pattern of rhythm or rhythms in lines of poetry; meter is the beat we can relate to just as in music. If you think of the poems you remember best, you might discover that they were rhythmical as well as rhymed. Critic John Middleton Murry wrote: "There is a background of metrical sameness separating us like a curtain from the practical world; there is a richness of rhythmical variation to make the world in which we are, worthy of attention." Rhythm is formed by the stress (or accent or beat) on certain syllables within what are called "feet" in lines of poetry. Some words are naturally stressed, others naturally not, so another function of diction is not only to select the right words to make the point of the poem, but to select the right ones with the right stress or lack thereof. In poetry written in English, the typical metrical feet are *iambic* ($\smile\,'$), *trochaic* ($'\smile$), *anapestic* ($\smile\smile\,'$), and *dactylic* ($'\smile\smile$). *Scansion* is the method of analyzing the kind of meter and number of feet used in a poetic line.

Ben Jonson's "Still to Be Neat," which follows, is an example of a rhythmical (and rhymed) poem containing precisely four feet in each line but with interesting metrical variation. Try "scanning" each line.

> Still to be neat, still to be drest,
> As you were going to a feast;
> Still to be pou'dred, still perfumed:
> Lady, it is to be presumed,
> Though arts hid causes are not found
> All is not sweet, all is not sound.
>
> Give me a look, give me a face,
> That makes simplicity a grace;
> Robes loosely flowing, hair as free:
> Such sweet neglect more taketh me,
> Than all th' adulteries of art.
> They strike mine eyes, but not mine heart.

You may wonder if Jonson is writing about Art or Woman—or both—here, but it is the striking control of meter that creates the rhythm that in the first place entraps us in the poem long enough to examine its theme.

Theme

As indicated in the section on fiction, theme is the essence of subject, which is more general. In that section, poet Wilfred Owen was contrasted with fiction writers Tolstoy and Hemingway. Here is another poet, perhaps the greatest, William Shakespeare, who within the constraints of the fourteen-line sonnet (number 116), addresses the durability of true love:

> Let me not to the marriage of true minds
> Admit impediments. Love is not love
> Which alters when it alteration finds,
> Or bends within the remover to remove:
> O, no; it is an ever-fixed mark,
> That looks on tempests and is never shaken:
> It is the star to every wandering bark,
> Whose worth's unknown, although his height be taken.
> Love's not Time's fool, though rosy lips and cheeks
> Within his bending sickle's compass come;
> Love alters not with his brief hours and weeks,
> But bears it out even to the edge of doom.
>   If this be error and upon me proved,
>   I never write, nor no man ever loved.

Themes in literature provide us with the tools we require for understanding a work. But theme is never stated; we arrive at it through action and insight when we have worked our way inside a story, novel, or poem.

INTERPRETING POETRY

When we say "work our way inside," we mean *knowing* a work of literature as well as we can. Reading and rereading a poem, aloud as well as silently, is one step to interpreting poetry. Another, as in fiction, is to know under what circumstances a poem was written. This, of course, additionally means knowing something about the author, and the more the better since, obviously, poems do not write themselves. Exercising your knowledge of the elements of poetry is a crucial factor in interpretation.

While there can be several interpretations of a work, there are always common elements that writers consider. Decide what kind of poetry is under discussion, dramatic monologue, lyric, or narrative (or a combination of them). Are you writing about closed poetry with its traditional rules, or open poetry which tends to make its own rules? Unlike a story, remember, a poem will render a great theme down to its essences, its most important aspects. Critical analysis requires that, early on in your paper, you state clearly what the theme is. Once you know that, you can then find the elements in the poem to support your opinion that the theme is what you think it is. If you are right, discuss the clues that led you to this conclusion, the words, the images, the lines and their formations.

Should your assignment be to compare two poems, the process is essentially the same. For example, given Shelley's "Ozymandias" and Coleridge's "Kubla Khan," you might arrive at somewhat similar themes that suggest, in sinister fashion, a warning to humankind. Both are set in unworldly locations; both possess an ominous, sometimes eerie tone, yet both are by lyrical poets, which means the poems are set in rhythm and rhyme. The most obvious point of *contrast,* on the other hand, is in the length of the two poems, the brevity of Shelley's, and the length and growth of power in Coleridge's.

Although Coleridge was born twenty years before Shelley, who drowned at 30, both were influenced by Wordsworthian ideals and the philosophies of the Age of Reason, which are other comparisons you can make. Coleridge died (at 62) but the lines in his "Kubla Khan" remain, as Rudyard Kipling said, "the most magical in the English language."

EVALUATING POETRY

If your instinct for liking what is good has served you well, trust it now. That is the starting place for evaluating a poem. A good poem should have meaning for you; it should make you think or wonder—and then think and wonder again about its content.

Not all poetry, however, is good, even if it has been published, but it still may be worthy of your consideration. If you examine rhythm or cadence in a closed or open poem, you should be critical of the poet's ability to maintain the beat; if it has broken down without any plausible reason, perhaps the poet tired of maintaining it, or forgot to. This failure might be one that caused you not to like the poem, though you may not have known the reason why.

If a poem has relied heavily on images you do not understand, or offers no hope whatsoever of being made clear, your evaluation will of course be negative, and rightly so. (Some poets work hard not to be understood.) Other poets, while seemingly accessible, are more subtle with the elements they employ, and you may find their work seductive. A poem with an abundance of metaphors or similes is one with too many images. On the other hand, a poem stingy with these and other elements that poetry requires may offer too little to engage you. Imprecise diction may echo like a wrong note played on a musical instrument, but recall that it was the precision of most of the diction that called your attention to the imprecision in the first place. Look for what bounces best off your own sensibilities, taking note of the advice suggested above. It may be worth knowing that for many poets, a poem remains an unfinished work; he or she will often go back to even an already published work in some cases and change something in it, which he or she believes will make it better. For most of us, good poetry makes us feel a way we cannot always explain other than to say, "good."

5

Writing about Drama

"All the world's a stage," wrote Shakespeare, and on that stage we witness the joys and sorrows, the tragedy and comedy, the reality and romance of life. While one traditional purpose of drama is to "suspend your sense of disbelief" so that you can respond emotionally to what you experience, thinking about and describing drama gives you a far deeper understanding of it. Learning about tragedy, comedy, tragicomedy, melodrama, and other types of plays will help you understand the conventions of dramatic literature and playwriting, and through this process, help you to not only experience the world of the play, but aid you in understanding *why* you experience it the way you do.

THE ELEMENTS OF DRAMA

Tragedy and comedy are the best known categories of dramatic writing perhaps because they were the first to be defined, and have a long, if somewhat erratic, tradition. Aristotle, in his *Poetics,* describes and defines the nature of tragedy, albeit his view was limited because he based it upon tragedy written during the "golden age" of Greek drama, and obviously could not foretell the evolution of the drama through the millennia to follow. But the prolific writings of Aeschylus, Sophocles, and Euripides—the three Greek tragedians whose plays remain extant—provided Aristotle with enough samples to devise a theory of tragic form. For Aristotle, tragedy focused on a hero (male or female) of noble birth, who, through a misdeed or *hamartia,* underwent a decline in stature that led to tragic consequences whether in the realm of material prosperity, physical well-being, or moral rectitude, or a combination of these, as in the case of *Oedipus Rex.* Even the titles of many Greek tragedies are the royal personages upon which the plays focus, such as *Antigone, Electra,* and *Agamemnon.*

The development and subsequent action of true tragedy usually derives from one or more of three possible modes of conflict: an internal conflict that the protagonist, or main character, must resolve within himself; a conflict between a protagonist and an outside antagonist; or one between the protagonist and the society-at-large. Although the play *A Raisin in the Sun* by Lorraine Hansberry might not be classified as a classic tragedy, it embodies all those conflicts that make tragedy possible. Walter Younger is confronted by several simultaneous conflicts. He is at odds with his family who have different ideas concerning how to spend his father's life insurance benefits. He is in conflict with society-at-large in the guise of Mr. Linder, who offers to buy back the home in a white neighborhood that the Younger family has just purchased, rather than allow the African-American family to move in. Finally, he must do battle with his own sense of righteousness and justice, whether to accede to the offer that will leave him with enough money to open his liquor store, and tacitly accept the racist motivation behind it; or keep the newly purchased house, and struggle to make a decent life for his family. Most drama that has been acknowledged through history as the finest examples of the playwright's art (such plays as *A Doll's House, Oedipus,* and *Death of a Salesman,* as well as most of the works of Shakespeare) interweave these three elements of conflict.

On the stage today, we rarely see a contemporary tragedy that rigidly conforms to the genre as it was first defined by Aristotle. First of all, few of us truly would be shocked by flaws in so-called great personages, as we have come to consider even the loftiest world leaders as human and subject to the same weaknesses as the rest of us. Tabloids are filled with sordid tales of great men and women and we have grown to take them for granted. Second, playwrights, beginning in the nineteenth century, have broadened their perspective to focus attention on the conflicts and actions of the lower and middle classes, not just the mighty and powerful. One might call this the democratization of tragedy, and this inclination has followed the same trends that have occurred in other art forms, for example, painting, poetry, architecture, and so on. Take for example the very name of the main protagonist in Arthur Miller's *Death of a Salesman*—where "Low-man" suggests his humble status.

Coinciding with the diminution in the stature of characters in drama has come a hybrid form that has come to be known as tragicomedy, that is, works of drama that combine the tragic and comic together. *A Raisin in the Sun* combines elements of both tragic and comic form as do David Hwang's *Family Devotions* and Susan Glaspell's *Suppressed Desires.* While these plays address issues such as intergenerational and intercultural conflict, rancor, jealousy, even murder, the playwrights have managed to inject moments of humor that add dimension to human experience.

We do not have a comprehensive theory of comedy from Aristotle (although he planned to write one), but we do have many early extant Greek comedies by the playwright Aristophanes who poked fun at Greek mores, politics, and society. Perhaps his most famous play is *Lysistrata,* which satirizes the absurdity of war as well as the "war between the sexes." Today, political satire is alive and well in film and television, and as you probably know, is a major subject for contemporary stand-up comedians.

The two Roman comic writers whose works are extant are Terence and Plautus. They helped to initiate the type of theater we know as comedy. Influenced by the Greeks, Plautus' plays satirized Roman life, using such devices as bungling behavior, reversals of expectations, and mistaken identity to keep his audience laughing. His most famous play, *The Menaechmi Twins,* was the inspiration for Shakespeare's first play, *The Comedy of Errors.* And today we still see the influence of Roman comedy in such forms as farce and slapstick in the theater and situation comedies on TV. Terence's comedies, on the other hand, did not go for the broad laugh, and just as is true among today's audiences, his more subtle comedies and humanistic themes were not as popular as Plautus', whose work inspired more belly laughs.

Melodrama is a type of drama which, although derived from tragedy, stands apart from it because the conflicts that the characters must confront are contrived or merely clever and the characters are usually less fleshed out than three-dimensional dramatic characters, and they seem to resolve their conflicts in interesting, yet concocted ways. While melodrama is not found as much on the stage today as it was in the nineteenth century, the form is alive and well in many contemporary action-adventure films like the *Indiana Jones* films and *Romancing the Stone,* where men and women are saved from disaster in the nick of time, much as they are in the old cliché of the damsel in distress who is tied to a railroad track as a speeding train approaches, only to be whisked away at the last moment by a valiant hero.

With the proliferation of drama portraying the common person, many audience members have become accustomed to associating plays with realistic portraits of life and with rather conventional ways of depicting such portraits, as though the theater were a place to see a mirror or reproduction of real life. This couldn't be further from the truth, however. Many so-called schools and movements of drama have depicted life in unrealistic manners. Playwrights such as Eugene Ionesco and Samuel Beckett portray a world that is quite unlike the one with which we are familiar. In your anthology, plays representing life with an unreal quality include depictions of life as romantic as in Lady Gregory's *The Rising of the Moon;* or absurd as in Samuel Beckett's *Krapp's Last Tape;* or magical as in Langston Hughes' *Soul Gone Home* and Estela Portillo's *Day of the Swallows.* Even the contemporary classic *Death of a Salesman* has many scenes of unreality, when, for example, Willie's brother seems to magically appear on stage much in the same way as the ghost appears in *Hamlet.*

Plot

As in fiction (short stories and novels) plot is essential to nearly all drama, in fact, possibly more so than to other forms of literature. Plot is a skeleton of the action in a play. It is what happens to characters under the circumstances the playwright has devised. One reason plot is so important in drama is that since plays are meant to be performed and seen, an audience will have little tolerance for pauses in the action. In fiction, on the other hand, action may be interwoven with physical description or character ruminations. In drama, what you see is what you get, so to speak. And it is the playwright, in his or her division of acts and scenes, who will determine the pauses in the action, whereas a reader is free to stop and start reading where he or she pleases.

To keep the plot of a drama interesting to its audience, most playwrights try to maintain a heightened level of action through the development of conflicts and obstacles that occur far more readily and densely than they do in real life. It is through such conflict that the plot moves forward. And the greater the stakes involved in these conflicts, the more riveting the play will be and the more you will care about how the conflict is resolved. Take for example, an early scene in *A Doll's House* by Henrik Ibsen. Nora, the protagonist, is having a discussion with Krogstad, a man from whom she borrowed money to keep her family intact during a stressful and tenuous period. Krogstad, a bank clerk, fearing that he will be passed by for a promotion by his superior, Helmer (Nora's husband), threatens to blackmail Nora by revealing that she borrowed money from him without her husband's knowledge.

KROGSTAD: ... My sons are growing up; for their sake, I must try to regain what respect-ability I can. This job in the bank was the first step on the ladder. And now your husband wants to kick me off that ladder into the dirt.

NORA: But my dear Mr. Krogstad, it simply isn't in my power to help you.

KROGSTAD: You say that because you don't want to help me. But I have the means to make you.

NORA: You don't mean you'd tell my husband that I owe you money?

KROGSTAD: And if I did?

NORA: That' be a filthy trick!

Nora counters that her husband will merely pay back the money that is owed, which would at first glance seem to defuse Krogstad's threat. But Krogstad retaliates and increases the stakes and the conflict by dangling a damaging secret about Nora's loan before her. Several lines later, the following exchange occurs:

KROGSTAD: I promised to get you the money in exchange for an I.O.U., which I drew up.

NORA: Yes, and which I signed.

KROGSTAD: Exactly. But then I added a few lines naming your father as security for the debt. This paragraph was to be signed by your father.

NORA: Was to be? He did sign it.

· · ·

KROGSTAD: Tell me, Mrs. Helmer, do you by any chance remember the date of your father's death? The day of the month, I mean.

NORA: Papa died on the twenty-ninth of September.

KROGSTAD: Quite correct; I took the trouble to confirm it. And that leaves me with a curious little problem—[*Takes a paper.*] which I simply cannot solve.

NORA: Problem? I don't see—

KROGSTAD: The problem, Mrs. Helmer, is that your father signed this paper three days after his death.

This building and relaxing and building again of tension is what moves the action of the play forward, giving shape to the plot.

While the building up of tension in this example is fairly clear, what seems to be mere conversation in a play often contains the seeds of conflict that will have an impact on the later action. This is particularly true of more contemporary plays that portray human action in subtler terms. Take for example one of the many conflicts that beset the Younger family in *A Raisin in the Sun*—the conflict between Walter's ambitions and the caution of his wife, Ruth. It is evident even in this bit of morning banter from Act I:

WALTER: You know what I was thinking 'bout in the bathroom this morning?
RUTH: No!
WALTER: How come you always try to be so pleasant?
RUTH: What is there to be pleasant 'bout?
WALTER: You want to know what I was thinking 'bout in the bathroom or not?
RUTH: I know what you thinking 'bout.
WALTER: 'Bout what me and Willy Harris was talking about last night.
RUTH: Willy Harris is a good-for-nothing loudmouth.

We eventually learn that Willy Harris is involving Walter in a scheme to open up a liquor store, and this has a dramatic impact on Walter's actions during the play, initiating a complex series of conflicts between himself and other members of his family.

While plays rely on rising action that is a result of tensions that in turn are caused by a conflict or a series of conflicts, this conflict must somehow be resolved or at least relieved in the end. It is unlikely that you would feel satisfied with a plot that left a major conflict unresolved. As in most plays, the climax to the rising action in *A Raisin in the Sun* occurs near its end. In this poignant scene, Walter's internal and external conflicts are resolved in a showdown with Mr. Linder when the latter pays his final visit to purchase back a house the Younger family has bought in a white neighborhood:

WALTER: Yeah, Well—what I mean is that we come from people who had a lot of *pride*. I mean—we are very proud people. And that's my sister over there and she's going to be a doctor—and we are very proud—
LINDER: Well—I am sure that is very nice, but—
WALTER: What I am telling you is that we called you over here to tell you that we are very proud and that this—Travis, come here. This is my son, and he makes the sixth generation our family in this country. And we have all thought about your offer—
LINDER: Well, good . . . good—
WALTER: And we have decided to move into our house because my father—my father—he earned it for us brick by brick. We don't want to make no trouble for nobody or fight no causes, and we will try to be good neighbors. And that's *all* we got to say about that. We don't want your money.

The Younger family's conflict now resolved, the play ends with them bantering happily about their move, their spirits uplifted. As you read a play, keep in mind the importance of plot and make notes on how the plot develops. To learn more about plot, you may also want to predict how the plot unfolds, and compare your idea with that of the author's.

Character

Aristotle suggested and playwrights in general follow the rule of thumb that "character is action." Another way of thinking about character is to envision him or her as determined by the choices he or she makes. Take the character of Iago from *Othello*. In the character list he is described as "IAGO, Othello's ensign, a villain." This does not tell us very much. However, in the first Scene of *Othello*, we soon find out what kind of person he is. Othello, it appears, has passed over Iago for promotion to lieutenant. Iago is enraged, for—as far as he is concerned—he has the greater experience in matters of war than the candidate Othello has demonstrated. He states his feelings to Roderigo this way:

> Preferment goes by letter and affection,
> And not by old graduation, where each second
> Stood heir to th' first. Now, sir, be judge yourself,
> Whether I in any just term am affined
> To love the Moor.

During the course of the play, Iago's character is revealed as he methodically torments Othello until the latter thinks Desdemona, his wife, has been unfaithful, resulting in the demise of both Othello and his wife. While most of us would like to take revenge upon a seemingly unfair boss, few of us would act upon it as Iago does. Understanding the traits that make character interesting is what allowed Shakespeare to appeal to an audience that was made up of all social classes. So, despite the fact that Shakespeare is renowned for the quality of his language, it is his talent for developing character that makes him a good playwright. This focus on the relationship between action and character should not give you the impression that a three-dimensional character is fully developed through his or her actions alone or that it is easy to develop a dramatic character. For a character to behave plausibly throughout a play, the playwright must have a strong sense of who that character is, how the character looks, sounds, dresses, thinks, reacts, and so on. Henrik Ibsen, one of the fathers of modern drama (perhaps because of his ability to create such well-motivated characters) said this about the people who inhabited his plays:

> Before I write down one word, I have to have the character in mind
> through and through, and I must penetrate into the last part of his soul—the indi-
> vidual comes before anything else—the stage set, etc. . . .

The most interesting characters in drama tend to be complex ones, and their actions although seemingly truthful may not necessarily be anticipated ones. Who would think that the Sergeant in Lady Gregory's *The Rising of the Moon* would let the fugitive go or that Othello would kill his wife or that Willy Loman, despite his pathetic nature, would kill himself so his family could be sustained by his insurance money, or that Oedipus would blind himself? All these actions are credible, but unexpected. In writing about character, ask yourself questions. Most likely they are the same sorts of questions the playwright asked as he or she planned to write. Who is this character? What are the given circumstances of time, place, social class, and situation that he or she must respond to? How does he or she respond?

Not all characters in plays are so fully developed that you will feel you know all about them. Many plays are populated by characters who enter the stage for a small portion of the play. These are often called "secondary characters." But a talented playwright will have even secondary characters. For example, Sylvester, Ma Rainey's nephew in August Wilson's *Ma Rainey's Black Bottom,* is fleshed out, interesting, and a contributing factor in the action of the play, having been endowed with a puerile personality and a noticeable stutter.

Setting

Unlike the movies, where you may be transported from New York to California to Tokyo in the blink of an eye, the settings in plays remain rather static throughout the action, changing perhaps between acts, if at all. And also unlike movies, which can actually show us all the minutiae of life by directly filming it, settings in drama often only suggest the places they depict, or, if it is in the playwright's vision, even distort them. Still other playwrights may not consider setting important at all, and their plays are often devoid of any description as to how the stage should be depicted, leaving it up to you, the reader or playgoer, to fill in the gaps with your imagination.

Besides revealing time and place through props (furniture, everyday objects, and costuming), setting can also exploit stage lighting and special effects such as rear-projected film and sound effects to enhance the mood of a play. Dim lighting might suggest a depressing atmosphere; bright lights, an upbeat one. Advances in theatrical technology have expanded the possibilities of establishing setting, as they have our expectations of how setting is depicted. The Greeks relied upon the simplest of means to suggest time and place—for example, a vertical rectangular box that was painted with a tree on one side, an architectural column on the other (which would be turned according to whether the scene was set in the city or the countryside). Contemporary playwrights, on the other hand, have often called for fairly elaborate staging so that the audience actually sees a fair representation of the place it is meant to depict. In the end, however, the complexity or lack thereof of a setting is usually up to the vision of the playwright. Notice, for example, the opening setting from the contemporary playwright David Hwang's *Family Devotions.*

> The sunroom and backyard of a home in Bel Air. Everywhere is glass—
> glass roof, glass walls. Upstage of the lanai/sunroom is a patio with a barbecue

and a tennis court. The tennis court leads offstage. As the curtain rises, we see a single spotlight on an old Chinese face and hear Chinese music or chanting. Suddenly, the music becomes modern-day funk or rock 'n' roll, and the lights come up to reveal the set. The face is that of DI-GOU, an older Chinese man wearing a blue suit and carrying an old suitcase. He is peering into the sunroom from the tennis court, through the glass walls. Behind him, a stream of black smoke is coming from the barbecue.

Another function of setting that may perform an important role in the life of a play is its ability to suggest the mood of the environment and/or reveal aspects of the character's or characters' interior emotions. Note Lorraine Hansberry's use of personification in her description of the Younger household at the start of *A Raisin in the Sun,* a description that provides you with an insight into the emotional tenor of the occupants.

> Its furnishings are typical and undistinguished and their primary feature now is that they have clearly had to accommodate the living of too many people for too many years—and they are tired. . . . Now the once loved pattern of the couch upholstery has *to fight to show itself* from under acres of crocheted doilies and couch covers . . . but the *carpet has fought back by showing its weariness,* with depressing uniformity, elsewhere on its surface.

Thus, the setting mirrors the Younger family's life circumstances and their interior lives as well, and at the same time provides an introduction to the play that may rivet your attention and make you want to read more.

The description of setting that introduces Arthur Miller's *Death of a Salesman* produces a similar effect in providing an analogy between Willy's home and its environs and Willy's state of mind in relationship to *his* environment. It is interesting to note that Miller's original title for the play was "The Inside of His Head."

> We are aware of towering, angular shapes behind it, surrounding it on all sides. Only the blue light of the sky falls upon the house and forestage; the surrounding area shows an angry glow of orange. As more light appears, we see a solid vault of apartment houses around the small, fragile-seeming home. An air of the dream clings to the place, a dream rising out of reality.

Staging

Plays are meant to be performed and for audiences to view the performances. If you've ever read a play and then gone to see it performed, you probably became aware of the difference between the two experiences. Seeing a performance of a play is what makes it complete. While you can ascertain certain things from reading plays that you would be hard pressed to do from a performance, for example, arcane references in the dialogue, subtleties of style, camouflaged symbols and the like, being present at a performance of a play adds a dimension to your understanding and appreciation of drama that is impossible from reading.

In staging a play, the theater artist has to consider such elements as casting, makeup, costume, the arrangement and movement of the actors on the stage (referred to as blocking), physical and vocal pacing, vocal qualities—in fact, nearly anything that contributes to communicating the world of the play to the mind of the audience member. While nothing can substitute for seeing a live performance, one way to envision what a play would be like performed when you read it is to imagine how you would see it at a performance. For example, how do you imagine Nora to look in *A Doll's House*? How does Othello or Oedipus carry himself? Is the former tall, short; does he possess a serious demeanor? How is the latter dressed? Oedipus is supposed to have a misshapen foot. How do you imagine him to walk? What sorts of miens do the musicians carry in *Ma Rainey's Black Bottom*? Do they appear angry, resigned, frustrated, etc.? It is important for you to consider that while a play in manuscript form is made up of words on a page, the stage is a physical and visual space that must be filled and kept interesting through props, costume, movement, activity, vocal character, lighting, and sound.

Dialogue

When you read a play, particularly a contemporary one like *A Raisin in the Sun* or *Ma Rainey's Black Bottom,* chances are you find the dialogue similar to everyday speech, which is casual, colloquial, and conversational. If so, the playwright is doing a good job at giving you the *illusion* that dialogue is like the daily conversations each of us has. Actually, good dialogue is distilled speech and is structured so that it consistently contributes to the creation or resolution of conflict, moving the action of the play forward, or enlightening us about character. What might appear to you as mere transposition of speech from a tape recorder to the page is actually a craft that requires a keen sense of language and its rhythms. A playwright may very well write and rewrite a play many times until he or she gets it right. One playwright, in a humorous mood, once offered a $10,000 reward for anyone who could show him a tape recorder that recorded dramatic dialogue from real life.

Read the following dialogue from *The Rising of the Moon* by Lady Gregory, and consider how it contributes to the drama:

POLICEMAN B: I think this would be a good place to put up a notice. [*He points to barrel.*]
POLICEMAN X: Better ask him. [*Calls to* SERGEANT.] Will this be a good place for a
   placard?

[*No answer.*]

POLICEMAN B: Will we put up a notice here on the barrel?

[*No answer.*]

SERGEANT: There's a flight of steps here that leads to the water. This is a place that should
   be minded well. If he got down there, his friends might have a boat to meet him; they
   might send it in here from outside.

POLICEMAN B: Would the barrel be a good place to put a notice up?
SERGEANT: It might; you can put it there.

[They pass the notice up.]

SERGEANT: [*Reading it.*] Dark hair-dark eyes, smooth face, height five feet five—there's not much to take hold of in that—It's a pity I had no chance of seeing him before he broke out of gaol. They say he's a wonder, that it's he makes all the plans for the whole organization. There isn't another man in Ireland would have broken gaol the way he did. He must have some friends among the gaolers.
POLICEMAN B: A hundred pounds is little enough for the Government to offer for him. You may be sure any man in the force that takes him will get promotion.
SERGEANT: I'll mind this place myself. I wouldn't wonder at all if he came this way.

In only a few sentences, this dialogue establishes a number of important dramatic issues. It establishes the locale. It provides us an understanding of the characters' motivations for their actions. It sets up the mood since the police reveal through their observations that they are in a strange part of the city, making their actions tentative. Their subordinate relationship to the sergeant, their supervisor, is established. Note too that there are pauses in the dialogue when the two police call and the sergeant does not respond. What do you think is implied by the fact that the sergeant does not respond? What do you think is implied by the fact that the sergeant does not answer them? How do the pauses contribute to the mood? Anton Chekhov, the great Russian playwright, used pauses in the dialogue to great psychological effect as did the modern playwright, Samuel Beckett (study *Krapp's Last Tape* for evidence of this).

Another function of a play's dialogue is exposition, which refers to the explanation or description of action, events, or people that are not revealed to us directly. So, for example, without even directly showing the fugitive the police are seeking in *The Rising of the Moon,* Lady Gregory, the playwright, informs us what he looks like when the sergeant reads the "wanted" poster. We also learn—without seeing—the fact that the water is close, providing a likely means for escape. What other things does exposition in the dialogue tell you? Unlike short stories and novels, where the narrator can describe events that have happened in the past or make you privy to the thoughts of a character, plays have only dialogue to serve these functions. A good playwright will interweave exposition into what is being said without your being aware of it. One exercise you might try to gain a better sense of the playwright's art is to study the way he or she employs exposition.

As stated before, dialogue is not merely recorded speech, yet critics often speak of a playwright as "having an ear" for dialogue. This usually means that the author seems to have a talent for imitating the tone, the rhythms of speech, and the regional and/or class dialects of the people he is portraying. Thus, while Cutler, Toledo, Slow Drag, and Levee are characters in a play, August Wilson's talent for rendering regional accents, dialect, and slang allows skilled actors to take what these characters say on the page and make it come alive, giving you the impression of real people.

Theme

Theme is a slippery topic in talking about drama as it is for any genre of literature. For it asks the questions, "What does the play mean?" or "What is the author trying to say?" Understanding the theme or themes of a play seen on a stage may be even more difficult than deciphering the meaning of other forms of literature, since often you will be emotionally carried along by the action, whereas in a novel or short story, you can always pause and consider the significance of what you have read. Although there is no hard and fast rule, it is perhaps in understanding theme that *reading* a play may have an advantage over *seeing* a play.

Sometimes the title of a play can offer a clue to its theme, as do the titles *A Doll's House, A Raisin in the Sun,* and *The Rising of the Moon.* (Note too that the latter two titles have images that have been traditionally used as symbols.) The phrase "a raisin in the sun" is from a poem by Langston Hughes that deplores the betrayal of the promise to provide African-Americans with equal rights; the phrase "rising of the moon" suggests an awakening of what is often repressed or suppressed from consciousness, the moon being a symbol in many cultures of the hidden aspect of human nature.

In Hansberry's play, you will find enacted among the characters the fight to achieve racial justice and the outcome of this fight for one family. In Lady Gregory's play, you find the Sergeant's attitude transform from one of an officious civil servant to a humane individual who gets in touch with his early roots and values. Thus *The Rising of the Moon* can be taken to be a statement about the suppression of the Irish independence movement as symbolized through the encounter between the Sergeant and the Ragged Man. The term "doll" as used in doll's house has meanings that go beyond the literal meaning of a child's plaything. In Ibsen's play, Nora seems to be treated as a doll by her husband, and her rebellion at the end is her escape from this unflattering and demeaning role.

Titles aside, themes in plays can be inferred through the study of other images, actions, and statements, particularly when they recur. When you read a play, be aware of such repetitions, and see if there seems to be a common thread that stitches them together. By this method you may be able to interpret motifs in what you read or see to more general or universal pronouncements about the human condition. Critics have noted the importance of Lena Younger's (Mama) plants in *A Raisin in the Sun* and interpret them as symbols for the determined survival of the Younger family. Other critics make much of the tape recorder in *Krapp's Last Tape,* suggesting that it represents the human experience, which is merely a playing out of what has already been recorded by consciousness, providing the dim view that humans have little say in determining their destinies.

To appreciate the full dimension of what you read, and to find hooks that can provide topics for discussion or writing, look for recurring motifs and character transformations in plays. These will more than likely lead you to discovering a play's theme.

INTERPRETING DRAMA

Interpreting plays, like interpreting other works of literature, is an elusive task. You, like your classmates, and readers in general, come to the specific work with your own background, prejudices, viewpoints, and attitudes. In addition, the time you live in, the place you live in, your cultural heritage: all have an impact on the meaning you extract from literature. To give just one superficial example, a salesman, after seeing a performance of Arthur Miller's play, *Death of a Salesman,* is reported to have said to his wife, "I always said the Northeast was a lousy sales territory." Whether his pragmatic response to the play was of the sort Miller wanted audience members to have is doubtful; yet, there are *many* possible valid interpretations of a play, not *the* one true interpretation.

Dramatic literature, perhaps more than other forms of literature, should make this indeterminate aspect of interpretation evident, since most plays are meant to be performed. Thus, even the performance of a play will alter the play's import, being influenced by the director's and actors' visions. Another aspect of plays which makes interpretation problematic is the fact that most plays that have lasting appeal are complex works of art, just as is the case with other forms of literature. Therefore, to tease out the meaning from what you read is not as simple as finding the right answer on a multiple choice test. It is rather like deciphering a secret code or putting together the pieces of a puzzle.

Since it is probably impossible to actually *prove* that your interpretation is the right one, it is better to think of interpretation as an argument, that is, as a statement that you will try to back up with evidence from what you have read or seen. And since plays that stand the test of time tend to be complex, it is perhaps better to develop an argument that addresses one aspect of a play rather than the entire play itself. Another reason for limiting your interpretation of a play is that if you select too broad an interpretation, it may be difficult to include all that you need to support your interpretation in a college-length paper. For example, consider the following interpretation of Miller's *Death of a Salesman:* "*Death of a Salesman* shows the tragic consequences of taking at face value the traditional concepts of 'the American dream' without questioning or considering their merits." While this interpretation is valid, it would be nearly impossible to discuss all the pertinent evidence that exists in the play that supports this theme, since the play is replete with images, dialogue, description, and relationships that advance it.

In reading a play carefully, try to find particular speeches, images, symbols, or statements that present a means of interpreting a particular aspect of the play. For example, character is one aspect of a play that deserves special attention, and to which interpretation can bring fruitful results. You may wish to select a character that interests you, intrigues you, or seems to possess a special quality that may be overlooked by a superficial reading of the play. Take for example one student who read August Wilson's play *Ma Rainey's Black Bottom.* Intrigued by the character of Toledo, he reread the text focusing on Toledo's relationships with the other band members, his philosophical statements and observations, and his action during the course of the play. He was particularly intrigued by a speech of his early in Act I:

TOLEDO: See, now . . . I'll tell you something. As long as the colored man look to white folks to put the crown on what he say . . . as long as he looks to white folks for approval . . . then he ain't never gonna find out who he is and what he's about. He's just gonna be about what white folks want him to be about. That's one sure thing.

Reviewing the play, the student then highlighted Toledo's dialogue and found a pattern that seemed to bear out the idea that Toledo was revealing certain truths about the African-American's dilemma in America, and that in a sense he becomes a martyr whose truth cannot be accepted by the other members of the band, and thus is killed in the end for his beliefs.

EVALUATING DRAMA

You may interpret the meaning of a play, the significance of a character, the function of setting, and the like, without ever engaging in probably the most common form of writing about drama: evaluating. Theater critics, whether writing for newspapers like *The New York Times,* magazines like *Newsweek,* television news shows, or radio primarily engage in evaluation. That is, while they may describe and summarize a play, their ultimate purpose is to relate to their audiences the quality of the play, whether it is a masterpiece, a terrible travesty of dramatic art, or something in between.

When you evaluate a play, you may not reach a large audience, but you will, at the least, help hone your own critical abilities, and develop for yourself a sense of what makes or does not make for good dramatic literature. Ultimately, evaluation is a subjective affair, but there are certain guidelines that can help you appreciate the quality of a play, whether or not you agree with its message.

The first thing you might do is ask yourself a series of questions that can guide you into understanding why you like or dislike a play. If it moves you emotionally, why? If you identify with the characters, which ones, and why? Even if the world of the play is foreign to you, that is, takes place at another time, in another culture, or among a class of people you are unfamiliar with, ask yourself whether you find any similarities between the world of the characters and the world you yourself have experienced or could imaginatively experience. While chances are you have never been in a war, do the relationships that occur among the characters in John Williams' *August Forty-Five* seem plausible considering the circumstances?

Once you've established your own relationship to the play, you have a base from which you may use more abstract criteria in your evaluation. Earlier in this chapter, continuous *action* was described as being an essential part of most drama. Does the action in the play you have read seem coherent and unified? Most students of literature find coherence and unity important characteristics in determining the quality of a work of literature. If a character acts in a way that seems foreign or implausible to his or her nature, the chances are that the playwright has not fleshed out his conception of just who the character is.

Since plays are nearly all dialogue, one important aspect of evaluating a play is the extent to which the dialogue sounds true. Do the characters speak as if they were real people? Can you distinguish their class, culture, age, and personality from the way they speak? Does the dialogue seem to imitate the rhythms of speech? If the answers to these questions are in the negative, they may have a bearing on the quality of the play.

Universality of appeal is another criterion upon which to evaluate a play. Why is it that plays written over 2000 years ago—for example, *Oedipus Rex* or *Lysistrata*—are still read and performed today? More than likely it is because the issues that these plays raise are still of concern to contemporary audiences. Or take for example, plays that seem to cross cultures successfully. *Death of a Salesman* was translated into Chinese and successfully performed in China, a country that does not even have the profession of salesman. Still, audiences found the play pertinent to their lives. Other issues to consider are whether the play presents its world in an interesting, complex, and original fashion. Most people would agree that the world is a complex place with multidimensional challenges. If a play reflects this world, it could hardly do so by being simplistic. Thus, in evaluating a play, another issue to consider is whether the world it depicts addresses the complexity of life. If it lacks this dimension, chances are the play will fade quickly away in your mind whereas a play replete with ideas will be one you can turn to again and again, only to discover more intriguing issues about its characters, meaning, and significance.

Nonetheless, two individuals using all these criteria can come to radically different evaluations about a play, as the following excerpts from reviews of two well-known drama critics reveal. Both were responses to a Lorraine Hansberry (author of *A Raisin in the Sun*) play entitled *Les Blancs*. The first is by John Simon writing in *New York Magazine*:

> . . . The result is unmitigated disaster. *Les Blancs* (the very French title in what is clearly a British African colony testifies to the utter confusion) is not only the worst new play on Broadway, of an amateurishness and crudity unrelieved by its sophomoric stabs at wit, it is also, more detestably, a play finished—or finished off—by white liberals that does its utmost to justify the slaughter of whites by blacks. . . . It is a malodorous, unenlightening mess.

The second is by Walter Kerr, writing for *The New York Times*:

> I urge you to see Lorraine Hansberry's . . . ranging, quick-witted, ruefully savage examination of the state of the African mind today. . . . Virtually all of *Les Blancs* is there on the stage, vivid, stinging, intellectually alive, and what is there is mature work, ready to stand without apology alongside the completed work of our best craftsmen. The language in particular is so unmistakably stage language

that . . . it achieves an internal pressure, a demand that you listen to it, that is quite rare on our stages today.

If professional critics can differ so radically in their evaluation of a play, you should rely on your own taste, informed by your growing knowledge of fiction, poetry, and drama, when judging any work of literature.

PART THREE

Literary Research

6

Writing Literary
Research Papers

A *literary research paper* is a report in which you synthesize information on a poem, play, work of fiction, or author, and contribute your own analysis and evaluation to the subject. Research writing is a form of problem solving. You identify a literary problem, form a hypothesis (an unproven thesis, theory, or argument), gather and organize information from various sources, assess and interpret data, evaluate alternatives, reach conclusions, and provide documentation.

Research writing for literature courses is both exciting and demanding. American essayist and novelist Joan Didion states, "The element of discovery takes place, in nonfiction, not during the writing but during the research." Nowhere is the interplay of the stages in the composing process more evident than in writing research papers. Prewriting is an especially important stage, for the bulk of your research and bibliographical spadework is done before you actually sit down to draft your report. Moreover, a full range of strategic thinking skills is required at every step of research writing. Here is where you sense the active, questioning, reflective activity of the mind as it confronts a problem, burrows into it, and moves through the problem to a solution, proof, or conclusion. Developing the ability to do literary research writing thus represents an integration of problem-solving and composing talents.

Research writing *should* be treated as a talent rather than a trial. Unfortunately, there are many misconceptions about it. Contrary to conventional wisdom, research does not begin boringly with the library card catalogue and end with the final period that you put on a bibliographic entry. (In fact, computerized library searches and word processing have taken the drudgery out of writing research papers.) Nor does research writing exclusively involve a reporting of information. All too often college writers tackle a research report as a cut-and-paste job. If they are sly plagiarists, they pirate information from various sources and offer it in their "own" words. If they are honest but uninspired, they create a bland and boring recitation of facts, filled with citations and bibliographic flourish. This documentary-style of research turns you into a drone, the artist of slick footnotes and slack ideas.

Research actually means the careful investigation of a subject in order to discover or revise facts, theories, or applications. Your purpose is to demonstrate how other researchers approach a problem—whether in literature or any other academic area—and how *you* treat that problem. A good research paper reveals a subtle blend of your own ideas and the attitudes or findings of others as well. In research writing you are dealing with ideas that are already in the public domain, but you are also making a contribution to knowledge.

RESEARCH WRITING: THEORY AND PRACTICE

When *your* ideas become the center of the research process rather than the ideas of others, the theory and practice of writing a literary research paper becomes dynamic instead of static. The standard advice offered in English handbooks for preparing a research paper is to find a subject and then assemble information from sources usually found in a library. This strategy does teach disciplined habits of work and thought, and it is a traditional way to conduct research for college courses. Yet, does conventional handbook theory match the practices of professional researchers?

Consider the following tasks:

- Evaluate critical responses to Anne Sexton's last book of poetry.
- Write an analysis of the impact of the South on Richard Wright's literary career.
- Investigate the scandal over Ezra Pound.
- Assess the effectiveness of Western responses to Conrad's *Heart of Darkness,* comparing them with Achebe's essay on Conrad's novella.
- Discuss the dramatic effectiveness of Aristotle's theories of drama on *Oedipus Rex* by Sophocles.
- Define feminist fiction, using at least three stories from your text as the basis for your research.
- Analyze the impact of class and caste on Faulkner's "A Rose for Emily."

Several observations can be made about how a professional researcher would view these projects. First, the researcher sees his or her subject as a *problem,* rather than a mere topic. Often the problem is authorized or designated by a collaborator, editor, or person in authority. The researcher has the task of developing or testing a hypothesis stemming from the particular problem: for example, whether or not critics think that Aristotle's theory of the theater is dramatically effective. *Hypothesis formation* is at the heart of professional research.

Second, the researcher often has to engage in primary as well as secondary research. Primary research relies on your analysis of the text as well as letters, manuscripts, and often materials written by the author. *Secondary research* relies on sources that comment on the primary sources. For example, a commentary by Irving Howe on William Faulkner's "A Rose for Emily" would be a secondary source. Primary sources are not necessarily more reliable than secondary sources. You must always evaluate the reliability of both your primary and secondary source material. A literary critic can misinterpret (much Faulkner scholarship is terrible), and critics love to disagree, forcing you to weigh evidence and research your own conclusions.

Third, all researchers face deadlines—a few days, a week, a month, or more. Confronted with deadlines, professional researchers learn to *telescope* their efforts in order to obtain information quickly. Common ways of scoping for literary scholars include telephoning; networking (using personal and professional contacts); computerized or automated bibliographical searching; and selected use of bibliographies (lists of articles on the topic with commentaries on each item), specialized indexes, review articles, current articles, and guides to organizations. These sources, many of which are found in the reference room of a library, permit the researcher to *jump* into the middle of a problem, rather than tread water in front of a card catalogue.

Finally, much professional researching does not fall neatly into one academic content area. Typically, it cuts *across* subjects and disciplines (for example, the project on Ezra Pound would cut across literature, history, politics, psychology, economics, and more). The interdisciplinary nature of many research projects creates special problems for the researcher, especially in the use of bibliographical materials, which *do* tend to be subject oriented. Good researchers know that they cannot be ghettoized into one subject like history or physics. Knowledge in the contemporary era tends increasingly toward interdisciplinary concerns, and you must develop the critical thought skills needed to operate effectively in an increasingly complex world of interrelationships.

Training, discipline, and strong critical thinking skills are necessary for any form of college research. Such research is not beyond your talents and abilities. Learn how to use the library selectively and efficiently, but also learn how to view the world outside of your library as a vast laboratory to be used fruitfully in order to solve your research problems.

STAGES IN THE RESEARCH PROCESS

More than any other form of college writing, the research paper evolves gradually through a series of stages. This does not mean you proceed step-by-step through a rigid series of phases. You know from our discussion of the writing process that the act of composing moves back and forth over a series of activities and that the actual act of writing is unique to the individual. For example, when approaching the literary research paper, some individuals prefer to write an essay on some problem or issue that they know well and *then* fill in the research component. Others are more cautious and conduct research before writing anything. Some writers take notes on note cards; some store information in their computers; others, in the tradition of the journalist, jot down information in looseleaf pads. And there are some writers who, with a good internal sense of organization and design, manage to get by with seemingly chaotic ramblings recorded on any scrap of paper available. Writers with little experience in developing research papers do have to be more methodical than experienced researchers, who streamline and adjust the composing process to the scope and design of their projects.

Allowing for the idiosyncrasies of writers, we nevertheless can agree that the literary research process tends to move through several interrelated stages or phases. These key phases can be outlined as follows:

Phase 1: Defining Your Objective

Choose a *researchable* topic.

Identify a *problem* inherent in the topic which gives you the reason for writing about the topic.

Examine the *purpose* or the benefits to be gained from conducting research on the topic.

Think about your *audience*. Make certain that you know how you are going to *limit* your topic.

Establish a working *hypothesis* to guide and control the scope and direction of your research.

Phase 2: Locating Your Sources

Decide on your *methodology*—the types or varieties of primary and secondary research you plan to conduct. Determine the method of collecting data.

Go to the library and skim a general article or conduct a computer search to *determine if your topic is researchable* and if your hypothesis will stand up.

Develop a *tentative working bibliography,* a file listing sources that seem relevant to your topic.

Review your bibliography and *reassess your topic and hypothesis.*

Phase 3: Gathering and Organizing Data

Obtain your sources, taking notes on all information related directly to your thesis.

Analyze and organize your information. Design a *preliminary outline* with a tentative thesis *if* your findings support your hypothesis.

Revise your thesis if the findings suggest alternative conclusions.

Phase 4: Writing and Submitting the Paper

Write a *rough draft* of the paper, concentrating on the flow of thoughts and on integrating research findings into the texture of the report.

Write a *first revision* to tighten organization, improve style, and check on placement of data. Prepare citations that identify the sources of your information. Assemble a Works Cited section (a list of sources consulted).

Type the manuscript using the format called for by the course, the discipline, or the person authorizing the research project. Make a copy of the report. Submit the typewritten original copy.

The research process involves thinking, searching, reading, writing, and rewriting. The final product—the research paper—is the result of your discoveries in and contributions to the realm of ideas about literature.

Defining Your Objective

The first step in report-writing about literature is to select a researchable topic. You certainly do not want to discover ten weeks into the course that the topic you selected for a 1500-word term paper will take you a book to handle adequately. Nor do you want to risk spending fruitless days and weeks researching a topic that doesn't have enough information on it. As in the Goldilocks tale, you are in quest of a topic that is *just right*—a topic that is appropriate in scope for your assignment, a topic that offers an adventure for you in the realm of ideas, and a topic that offers interest, if not excitement, for your audience.

You reduce wasted time and effort if you approach the research project as a problem to be investigated and solved, a controversy to take a position on, or a question to be answered. At base, you need a strong hypothesis or working thesis (which may be little more than a hunch or a calculated guess). The point of your investigation is to identify, illustrate, explain, argue, or prove that thesis. *Start with a hypothesis* before you actually begin to conduct research; otherwise, you will discover that you are simply reading in or about a topic, instead of reading toward the objective or substantiating your thesis or proposition.

Of course, before you can formulate a hypothesis, you need to start with a general idea of what subject you want to explore, what your purpose is going to be, and how you plan to select and limit a topic from the larger subject area. Here, our earlier discussion of prewriting strategies for finding and limiting topics should be reviewed. At the same time, you should know that a topic lends itself to research and to hypothesis formation if 1) it is of strong interest to you, 2) you already know something about it, 3) it raises the sort of questions that require primary and secondary research in the library, and 4) you already have formed some opinions about various problems related to it. If you are free to choose your topic and you are expert in the poetry of Langston Hughes, it will be relatively easy to arrive at a strong, working thesis to serve as the basis for a rewarding research effort. If, on the other hand, a professor assigns a topic, one which you know little or nothing about, you might have to do some background reading before you can develop your hypothesis.

The trick at the outset of the research process is to fit your topic and hypothesis to the demands of the assignment. Your purpose is to solve a *specific* problem, shed light on a *specific* topic, state an opinion on a *specific* controversy, offer *specific* proofs or solutions. Your audience does not want a welter of general information, a bland summary of the known and the obvious, or free associations or meditations on an issue or problem. You know that your audience wants answers, and consequently a way to locate your ideal topic is to ask questions about it.

You may want to ask a series of specific questions about your subject and ultimately combine related questions. Remember to ask your questions in such a way as to pose problems that demand answers. Then try to determine which topic best fits the demands of the assignment and which lends itself to the most fruitful and economical method of library research.

Locating Your Sources

You have only a certain amount of time in which to locate information for any research project. If you have a sufficiently narrowed topic and a working hypothesis, you at least know what type of information will be most useful for the report. Not all information on a topic is relevant for your purposes; with a hypothesis you can distinguish between useful and irrelevant material.

To use your time efficiently you have to *streamline* your method for collecting data. Most report writing for college courses relies heavily on secondary research material in libraries. To develop a preliminary list of sources, you should go to general reference works if you have to do background reading or go directly to those resources that permit you to find a continuing series of articles and books on a single issue. Again, you should be moving as rapidly as possible from the general to the specific.

Checking General Reference Sources General reference sources include encyclopedias, dictionaries, handbooks, atlases, biographies, almanacs, and yearbooks. They can be useful for background reading and may give you some information on your topic. They may give you a few biographical hints, but the bibliographies they contain (as at the end of an article in an encyclopedia) are generally limited and frequently out of date. If you want to be a professional researcher, you should not rely on them exclusively to solve your research problems. Here are some standard reference works on literature and film that you will find in most libraries.

Adelman, Irving, and R. Dworkin. *Modern Drama: A Checklist of Critical Literature on Twentieth Century Plays.* 1967.
Altick, Richard, and Andrew Wright. *Selected Bibliography for the Study of English and American Literature.* 1979.
Bukalski, Peter J. *Film Research: A Critical Bibliography.* 1972.
Byer, Jackson, ed. *Sixteen Modern American Authors: A Survey of Research and Criticism.* 1973.
Cambridge History of English Literature. 15 vols. 1907–33.
Cassell's *Encyclopedia of World Literature.* Rev. ed. 1973.
Cawkwell, Tim, and John Milton Smith, eds. *World Encyclopedia of the Film.* 1972.
Contemporary Literary Criticism. 1976.
Etheridge, J. M., and Barbara Kopala. *Contemporary Authors.* 1967.
Hart, J. D. *Oxford Companion to American Literature.* 4th ed. 1965.
Hartnoll, Phyllis. *The Oxford Companion to the Theatre.* 3rd ed. 1967.
Harvey, Sir Paul, and J. E. Heseltine. *Oxford Companion to Classical Literature.* 2nd ed. 1937.
———. *Oxford Companion to English Literature.* 4th ed. 1967.
Hoffman, Daniel, ed. *Harvard Guide to Contemporary American Writing.* 1979.
Hornstein, Lillian H., ed. *The Reader's Companion to World Literature.* Rev. ed. 1973.
International Encyclopedia of the Film. 1972.
Kunitz, S. J., and Vineta Colby. *European Authors, 1000–1900.* 1967.
Kunitz, S. J., and Howard Haycraft. *American Authors, 1600–1900.* 1952.
———. *British Authors Before 1800.* 1952.
———. *British Authors of the Nineteenth Century.* 1936.
———. *Twentieth Century Authors.* 1942. Supplement, 1955.
Literary History of England. 2nd ed. 4 vols. 1967.
Literary History of the United States. 4th ed. 2 vols. 1974.
Manly, John M., and Edith Rickert. *Contemporary British Literature.* 1974.
Matlaw, Myron. *Modern World Drama: An Encyclopedia.* 1972.
Millett, Fred B. *Contemporary American Authors.* 1970.
New Cambridge Bibliography of English Literature. 4 vols. 1969–74.
New York Times Film Reviews. 1913–1968. 1970–71.
Walker, Warren S. *Twentieth Century Short Story Explanation.* 1977.
Whitlow, Roger. *Black American Literature.* 1973.
Woodress, James, ed. *American Fiction 1900–1950: A Guide to Information Sources.* 1974.
(For a comprehensive description of most indexes, see the *Bibliographic Index: A Cumulative Bibliography of Bibliographies.*)

Citation Indexes If you are interested in current research on a topic, you might want to use a citation index. This type of index gives the first time an important article appears and then lists later citations of the article or author in the scholarship of the field. The important citation indexes are:

Humanities Citation Index
Science Citation Index
Social Sciences Citation Index

Annual Reviews Summaries of important articles are collected in annual reviews for some fields of scholarship. Each year a group of professionals in a field, say, English, writes essays providing an overview of key topics in the area and what has been published about them. If your research topic is in an area covered by an annual review, this bibliographical source will prove of immense value. The standard annual reviews for literature are *Year's Work in English Studies* and *MLA International Bibliography of Books and Articles on Modern Language and Literature.*

Ask the reference librarian if there is an annual review that might be relevant to your research topic.

Using the Card Catalogue The library card catalogue consists of three files; these files list information by author, title, and subject. Of the three, the subject catalogue is the best place to look for sources, but it is *not* the place to start your research. A card catalogue is only as good as its library and the cataloguers in it. Moreover, despite the best efforts, a card catalogue is never up-to-date. In fact, current research is never reflected in a card catalogue. For this type of information you must rely on indexes, primary documents, and computer searches of articles.

The subject index can be useful when you are researching a topic around which a considerable body of information and analysis has already developed. A typical entry in the subject catalogue will look like this:

Check as many subject classifications that might be relevant to your topic as possible.

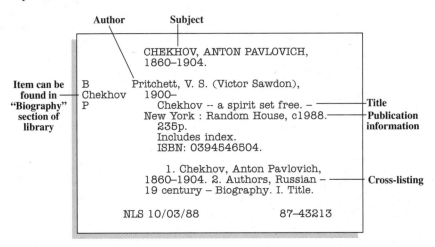

Preparing a Working Bibliography As you search for relevant articles and books, you should take down complete information on each item on 3 × 5 inch note cards or start a bibliographic file on your computer. Complete information, properly recorded, will save you the trouble of having to scurry back to the library for missing data when typing your final bibliography. Use a separate card for each entry that you think is promising, and keep your stack in alphabetical order.

Record the following information for a book:

Name(s) of author(s)
Title of book, underlined
Place of publication
Publisher's name
Date of publication
Call number

Record the following information for an article in a periodical:

Name(s) of author(s)
Title of article, in quotation marks
Title of periodical, underlined
Volume number
Date of publication
Numbers of pages on which article appears
Call number or location in library

List the call number or the location in the library so you can find the material once you are ready to begin reading and if you need to refer to it a second time.

In preparing a working bibliography, you should include all sources that you have a hunch are potentially useful. You may not be able to obtain all the items listed and some material will turn out to be useless, repetitious, or irrelevant to your topic, but it is easy to eliminate cards from your bibliography at a later stage. Your working bibliography will be longer than your final bibliography, which is called the Works Cited section.

When preparing bibliography cards for entries listed in annotated bibliographies, citation indexes, and abstracts, you might want to jot down any pertinent summaries that are provided.

One way to simplify the task of preparing your final Works Cited section is to use standard bibliographical form when doing your bibliography cards. The models given here are based on guidelines in the *MLA Handbook* (New York: 1988); they are usually followed in humanities research writing and generally accepted for college reports in the social sciences. Instructors in the social sciences and natural sciences (as well as in education and business) might want you to follow the *Publication Manual of the American Psychological Association* (2nd ed., 1975) or another style. Check with your instructors to determine which format they prefer. Also add both of these manuals to your own personal reference library.

Book with one author	Clark, Kenneth. *What Is a Masterpiece?* London: Thames and Hudson, 1979.
Two or more books by one author	Clark, Kenneth. *Feminine Beauty.* New York: Rizzoli, 1980.
	———. *What Is a Masterpiece?* London: Thames and Hudson, 1979.
Book with two or three authors	Gilbert, Sandra M., and Susan Gubar. *The Madwoman in the Attic: The Woman Writer and the Nineteenth Century Literary Imagination.* New Haven: Yale Univ. Press, 1979.
Book with more than three authors (editors)	Edens, Walter, et al., eds. *Teaching Shakespeare.* Princeton: Princeton Univ. Press, 1977.
Anonymous book	*A Visual Dictionary of Art.* Greenwich, Conn.: New York Graphic Society, 1974.
Work in a collection of pieces all by same author	Malamud, Bernard. *The Assistant.* In *A Malamud Reader.* New York: Farrar, 1967. 750–95.
Work in a collection of pieces by different authors	Hansberry, Lorraine. *A Raisin in the Sun.* In *Black Theatre: A Twentieth Century Collection of the Work of Its Best Playwrights.* Ed. Lindsay Patterson. New York: Dodd, Mead, 1971. 221–76.
Collection of pieces cited as a whole	Buell, Victor P., ed. *Handbook of Modern Marketing.* New York: McGraw-Hill, 1970.
Work in several volumes	Cassirer, Ernest. *The Philosophy of Symbolic Forms.* Trans. Ralph Manheim. 3 vols. New Haven: Yale Univ. Press, 1955.
Translation	Garcia Marquez, Gabriel. *Leaf Storm and Other Stories.* Trans. Gregory Rabassa. New York: Harper & Row, 1972.
Article in a reference book	"Mandarin." *Encyclopedia Americana.* 1980 ed.
Government publications	*Cong. Rec.* 7 Feb. 1973: 3831–51.
	United Nations. Center National Resouces, *State Petroleum Enterprises in Developing Counties.* Elmsford, N.Y.: Pergamon, 1980.
	Dept of Labor, Bureau of Statistics. *Dictionary of Occupational Titles.* 4th ed. Washington, D.C.: GPO 1977.
Legal reference	15 U.S. Code. Sec. 78j(b). 1964.
Article in a journal with continuous pagination through each volume	Spear, Karen. "Building Cognitive Skills in Basic Writers." *Teaching English in the Two-Year College* 9 (1983): 91–98.
Article in a journal with continuous pagination through each issue	Barthelme, Frederick. "Architecture." *Kansas Quarterly.* 13. 3–4 (1981): 77–80.

Article in a weekly or biweekly periodical	Begley, Sharon. "A Healthy Dose of Laughter." *Newsweek* 4 Oct. 1982: 74.
Article in a monthly or bimonthly periodical	Tucker, W. Henry. "Dilemma in Teaching Engineering Ethics." *Chemical Engineering Progress* Apr. 1983: 20–25.
Article in a daily newspaper	Brody, Jane. "Heart Attacks: Turmoil Beneath the Calm." *New York Times* 21 June 1983, late ed.: sec. 1.1 +.
Anonymous article	"Portents for Future Learning." *Time* 21 Sept. 1981: 65.
Review	Updike, John. "Cohn's Doom." Rev. of *God's Grace,* by Bernard Malamud. *New Yorker* 8 Nov. 1982: 167–70.
Lecture, speech, address	Ciardi, John. Address at Opening General Session. National Council of Teachers of English Convention, Washington, D.C. 19 Nov. 1982.
Film, slides, videotape	Chaplin, Charles, dir. *Modern Times.* With Chaplin and Paulette Goddard. United Artists, 1936.
	Creation vs. Evolution: "Battle of the Classroom." Videocassette. Dir. Ryall Wilson. PBS Video, 1982. (58 min.)
Radio and television programs	*The Life and Adventures of Nicholas Nickleby.* By Charles Dickens. Adapt. David Edgar. Dir. Trevor Nunn and John Caird. With Roger Rees and Emily Richard. Royal Shakespeare Co. Mobile Showcase Network. WNEW, New York. 10–13 Jan 1983.
Recording	Holiday, Billie. "God Bless the Child." Rec. 9 May 1941. *Billie Holiday: The Golden Years.* Columbia, C3L 21, 1962.
Computer software	Peterson, Terry. *HES MON.* Computer Software. Human Engineered Software, 1982. (VIC 20, cartridge/cassette).
Letter	Copland, Aaron. Letter to the author. 17 May 1982.
	Thackeray, William Makepeace. "To George Henry Lewes." 6 Mar. 1848. Letter 452 in *Letters and Private Papers of William Makepeace Thackeray.* Ed. Gordon N. Ray. Cambridge: Harvard Univ. Press, 1946. 2:353–54.
Interview	Gordon, Suzanne. Interview. *All Things Considered.* National Public Radio. 1 June 1983.

The purpose of compiling a bibliography is to keep track of where information is for additional reference, to determine the nature and extent of the information, to provide a complete and accurate list of sources to be presented in the paper, and to make preparing the final bibliography manuscript much easier.

Reassessing Your Topic Once you have compiled your working bibliography, take the time to reassess the entire project before you get more deeply involved in it. Analyze your bibliography cards carefully to determine whether you should proceed to the next stage of information gathering.

Your working bibliography should send out signals that help you to shape your thinking about the topic. The dominant signal should indicate that your topic is not too narrow or too broad. Generally, a bibliography of ten to fifteen promising entries for a 1500-word paper indicates that your topic might be properly limited at this stage. A listing of only three or four entries signals that you must expand the topic or consider discarding it. Conversely, a hundred note cards warn that you might be working yourself into a research swamp.

Another signal radiating from your working bibliography should tell you that your hypothesis is on target or that it can be easily recast to make it more precise. Entry titles, abstracts, and commentaries on articles are excellent sources of confirmation. If established scholarship does not support your hypothesis that Shakespeare did not write the plays attributed to him or that Ezra Pound was not a fascist sympathizer during World War II, it would be best to discard your hypothesis.

Finally, the working bibliography should provide signals about the categories or parts of your research. Again, titles, abstracts, and commentaries are useful. In other words, as you compile the entries you can begin to think through the problem and to perceive contours of thought that will dictate the organization of the paper even before you begin to do detailed research.

Your working bibliography should be alive with such signals.

Gathering and Organizing Data

If your working bibliography confirms the value, logic, and practicality of your research project, you can then move to the next phase of the research process: taking notes and organizing information. Information shapes and refines your thinking; you move from an overview to a more precise understanding, analysis, and interpretation of the topic. By the end of the third phase, you should be able to transform your hypothesis into a thesis and your assembled notes into an outline.

Your preliminary task as you move into the third phase is to immerse yourself in articles, books, and perhaps primary research sources, but *not* to drown in them. Begin by *skimming* your sources. Skimming is not random reading or casual perusal, but a careful examination of the material to sort out the valuable sources from the not-so-valuable. For books, check the table of contents and index for information on your topic, and then see if the information is relevant to your problem. For articles, see if the abstract or topic sentences in the body of the essay confirm your research interests.

The value of a source for your project is determined by the following criteria:

It must be directly relevant to your topic.
It should discuss the topic extensively.
It should bear on your hypothesis, either supporting or contradicting it.
It should present relatively current information, especially for research in the social and natural sciences.

Once you have a core of valuable source material, you can begin to read these sources closely and take detailed notes.

Note Taking Skillful note-taking requires a subtle blend of critical thinking skills. It is not a matter of recording all the information available or simply copying long quotes. You want to select and summarize the general ideas that will form the outline of your paper, to record specific evidence to support your ideas, and to copy exact statements you plan to quote for evidence or interest. You also want to add your own ideas and evaluation of the material. All the notes that you take must serve the specific purpose of your paper as it is stated in your hypothesis.

Take brief and precise notes. Look for the crisp quotation, the telling statistic, the insight by a leading authority, the sound original idea. Always keeping your hypothesis in mind will limit your note taking.

The best way to take notes is on 5 × 8 inch note cards. In preparing these cards, observe the following guidelines:

1. Write the author's name, title, and page number on each card. (Complete information on the source should already have been put on a bibliography card.)
2. Record only one idea or a group of closely related facts on each card.
3. List subtopics at the top of each card. This will permit you to arrange your cards from various sources into groups, and these groups can then serve as the basis of your outline.
4. List three types of information on your cards: a) summaries of material (see page 11); b) paraphrases of material, in which you stick more closely to the exact words of the author; c) *direct quotations,* accurately transcribed.
5. Add your own ideas at the bottom of the card.

The sample note card printed below indicates a good arrangement of research information.

Author of   Relevant
book or article   page numbers

Pritchett	*pp. 180–86*

Direct quote — *182: "Unlike later novelists, Chekhov never describes the sexual act."*

Student's commentary — *(yet the story does have an erotic mood.)*

Paraphrase — *186: Acc. to Pritchett, Chekhov once said it is not the function of art to solve problems but to present them correctly.*

Student's commentary — *(relate to ending of story.)*

When you have completed all of your research, organize your notes under the various subtopics or subheadings that you have established. If possible or desirable, try to combine some subtopics and eliminate others so that you have between three and five major categories for analysis and development. You are now ready to develop an outline for the research essay.

Designing an Outline   Because you must organize a lot of material in a clear way, an outline is especially valuable in a research essay. Some experts actually recommend that you develop an outline *before* you conduct research, but this is possible only if your bibliographical search and your own general knowledge of the topic permit establishing subtopics at that early stage.

Most importantly, now is the time to establish your thesis. By reviewing your note cards and assessing the data, you should be able to transform that calculated guess that was your hypothesis into a much firmer thesis.

Spend as much time as you think it is worth on drafting an outline. For a rough outline you can simply list your general subheadings and their supporting data. However, the recommended strategy is to work more systematically through your notes and compile as full an outline as possible, one that develops each point logically and in detail.

If you are required to submit an outline with your research paper, you should begin to develop a full, formal outline at this stage. Such an outline would look like this:

I. _____
   A. _____
   B. _____
      1. _____
      2. _____
      3. _____
         a. _____
         b. _____

Use Roman numerals for your most important points, capital letters for the next most important points, Arabic numbers for supporting points, and lower-case letters for smaller items.

Writing and Submitting the Paper

As you enter the fourth and final phase of the research process keep in mind that a research paper *is* a formal essay, not a jagged compilation of notes. You should be prepared to take your research effort through several increasingly polished versions, most likely at least a rough draft, a revised draft, and a final manuscript.

The Rough Draft For your rough draft, concentrate on filling in the shape of your outline. If your note cards have become skewed in order or scattered to the four corners of your room, take the time to rearrange them in the topic order that your outline assumes. In this way you will be able to integrate notes and writing more efficiently and effectively.

Even as you adhere to your formal outline in beginning the rough draft, you should also be open to better possibilities and prospects for presenting ideas and information. Often you discover that an outline is too rigid, that a minor idea needs greater emphasis, that something important has been left out entirely, even that your thesis needs further adjustment. There are potentially dozens of shifts, modifications, and improvements that you can make as you transfer the form of an outline to an actual written paper. Although your primary effort in writing a first draft is to rough out the shape and content of your paper, the flow of your ideas will often be accompanied by self-adjusting operations of the mind aimed at making your research effort even better than you thought it could be at the outline stage.

Whether or not you incorporate quotations from your notes into the rough draft is a matter of preference. Some writers prefer to transcribe quotations and paraphrases at this point in order to save time at a later stage. Other writers feel their thought processes are interrupted by having to copy quoted and paraphrased material and to design transitions between their own writing and the transcribed material. They simply write ''insert'' in the draft with a reference to the appropriate note card.

One test of your reasoning ability during the writing of the rough draft is the need to integrate material from several sources. For any given subtopic in your outline, you will be drawing together information from a variety of sources. To an extent, your outline will tell you how to arrange some of this information. At the same time, you must contribute your own commentary, arrange details in an effective order, and sort out conflicting claims and interpretations. A great deal of thinking as well as writing goes into the design of your first draft.

For now you simply want to express yourself clearly. At the same time you want to adhere to the standards of essay form, reasoning, and style that determine the quality of your writing.

It is critical thinking and problem solving as much as the act of writing that makes for a successful rough draft. You are actually in the process of solving a complex research problem in your own words. Although for now you do not have to worry about the polished state of your words, you do have to be certain that the intelligence that you are bringing to bear on the design of your paper is adequate to the challenge. You are not involved in a dull transcription of material when writing the rough draft of a research paper. Instead, you are engaged in a demanding effort to think your way through a problem of considerable magnitude, working in a logical way from the introduction and the statement of your thesis, through the evidence, to the outcome or conclusion that supports everything that has come before.

The Revised Draft   If you can put your rough draft away for a day or two, you can return to it with the sharpened and objective eye of a critical reviewer. In the rough draft you thought and wrote your way through the problem. Now you must *re*think and *re*write in order to give better form and expression to your ideas.

Use the guidelines outlined below to approach your revision. Consider every aspect of your paper, from the most general to the most specific. Look again at the organization of the whole essay, key topics, paragraphs, and sentences; read through for clarity of expression and details of grammar, punctuation, and spelling.

Here is a checklist to guide your revision:

1. Does my title illuminate the topic of the essay and capture the reader's interest?
2. Have I created the proper tone to meet the expectations of my audience?
3. Does my opening paragraph hook the reader? Does it clearly establish and limit the topic? Is the thesis statement clear, limited, and interesting?
4. Do all of my body paragraphs support the thesis? Is there a single topic and main idea for each paragraph? Do I achieve unity, coherence, and proper development? Is there sufficient evidence in each paragraph to support the main idea?
5. Are there clear and effective transitions linking my ideas within and between paragraphs?

6. Have I selected the best strategies to meet the demands of the assignment and the expectations of my audience?
7. Are all of my assertions clearly stated, defined, and supported? Do I use sound logic and avoid faulty reasoning? Do I acknowledge other people's ideas properly?
8. Is my conclusion strong and effective?
9. Are my sentences grammatically correct? Have I avoided errors in verbs, agreement, pronouns, adverbs, adjectives, and prepositions?
10. Are my sentences complete? Have I corrected all fragments, comma splices, and run-ons?
11. Have I varied my sentences effectively? Have I employed clear coordination and subordination? Have I avoided awkward constructions?
12. Is my use of periods, commas, semicolons, and other forms of punctuation correct?
13. Are all words spelled correctly? Do my words mean what I think they mean? Are they specific? Are they concrete? Is my diction appropriate to college writing? Is the diction free of clichés, slang, jargon, and euphemisms? Do I avoid needless abstractions? Is my usage sound?
14. Have I carefully attended to such mechanical matters as apostrophes, capitals, numbers, and word division?
15. Does my manuscript conform to acceptable guidelines for submitting type-written work?

A comprehensive revision effort will result in a decidedly more polished version of your paper.

Documentation   Documentation is an essential part of any research paper. Documenting your sources throughout the paper and in Works Cited tells your audience just how well you have conducted your research effort. It offers readers the opportunity to check on authorities, to do further reading, and to assess the originality of your contribution to an established body of opinion. Neglect of proper documentation can destroy your research effort. It can also be *plagiarism*—the use of material without giving credit to the source, or, put more seriously, the theft of material that properly belongs to other thinkers, writers, and researchers.

Quotations and paraphrases obviously require credit, for they are the actual words or the theories or interpretations of others. Paraphrases and summaries also frequently offer statistics or data that are not well-known, and this type of information also requires documentation. Facts in a controversy (facts open to dispute or to varying interpretations) also fall within the realm of documentation. In summary, documentation is needed for:

1. Direct quotations;
2. Paraphrased material;
3. Any key idea or opinion adapted and incorporated into your material;

4. Specific data (quoted, paraphrased, tabulated);
5. Disputed facts

The most common method of indicating sources is parenthetical documentation within the text. The author's last name and the page number in the source are given in parentheses where the material occurs in your paper. Complete information is listed, alphabetically by author, in the Works Cited section. The information on your bibliography cards should provide you with the details needed for the preparation of parenthetical documentation.

For parenthetical documentation:

1. Give enough information so that the reader can readily identify the source in the Works Cited.
2. Give specific information, especially when dealing with multivolume works, editions, newspapers, and the law.
3. Make certain that the complete sentence containing the parenthetical documentation is *readable* and grammatically correct.

There is considerable variety in the form of citation of sources from field to field. The following models for parenthetical documentation are based on the *MLA Handbook* cited earlier.

Type of Citation	Text and Parenthetical Documentation	Form in Works Cited Section
Page numbers of a one-volume work	Another particularly appealing passage is the opening of the story "A Very Old Man with Enormous Wings" (Garcia Marquez 105).	Garcia Marquez, Gabriel. "A Very Old Man with Enormous Wings." In *Leaf Storm and Other Stories.* Trans. Gregory Rabassa. New York: Harper & Row, 1972. 105–12.
	Hansberry offers what many audiences have found a satisfying conclusion (265–76).	Hansberry, Lorraine. *A Raisin in the Sun.* In *Black Theatre: A Twentieth Century Collection of the Work of Its Best Playwrights.* Ed. Lindsay Patterson. New York: Dodd, Mead, 1971. 221–76.
Volume and page numbers of a multivolume work	Interest in Afro-American literature in the 1960s and 1970s inevitably led to "a significant reassessment of the aesthetic and humanistic achievements of black writers" (Inge, Duke, and Bryer 1:v).	Inge, M. Thomas, Maurice Duke, and Jackson Boyer, eds. *Black American Writers: Bibliographic Essays.* 2 vols. New York: St. Martin's, 1978.

Type of Citation	Text and Parenthetical Documentation	Form in Works Cited Section
Page and column numbers of a newspaper article	A 1983 report found "a decline in the academic quality of students choosing teaching as a career" (Hook 10, col. 5).	Hook, Janet. "Raise Standards of Admission, Colleges Urged." *Chronicle of Higher Education* 4 May 1983: 1, col. 4 +.
Work listed by title	*Computerworld* has developed a thoughtful editorial to the issue of government and technology ("Uneasy Silence" 54), and one hopes such public discussion will continue in the future.	"An Uneasy Silence." Editorial. *Computerworld* 29 Mar. 1983: 54.
Work by a corporate author	The Commission on the Humanities has concluded that "the humanities are inescapably bound to literacy" (69).	Commission on the Humanities. *The Humanities in American Life: Report of the Commission on the Humanities.* Berkeley: Univ. of California Press, 1980.
Two or more works by the same author(s)	In *The Age of Voltaire* the Durants portray eighteenth-century England as a "humble satellite" in the world of music and art (214–48). To Will and Ariel Durant, creative men and women make "history forgivable by enriching our heritage and lives" (Dual Autobiography 406).	Durant, Will, and Ariel Durant. *The Age of Voltaire.* Vol. 9 of *The Story of Civilization.* New York: Simon & Schuster, 1965. ———. *A Dual Autobiography.* New York: Simon & Schuster, 1977.
Indirect sources	Samuel Johnson admitted Edmund Burke was an "extraordinary man" (qtd. in Boswell 2: 450).	Boswell, James. *The Life of Johnson.* Ed. George Birkbeck Hill and L. F. Powell. 6 vols. Oxford: Clarendon, 1934–50.

The author-date system of documentation, common to the social and physical sciences, adds the *date of publication* to the standard parenthetical information:

> In *The Age of Voltaire* the Durants portray eighteenth-century England as a "humble satellite" in the world of music and art (1965, 214–48).

The author-date system requires an adjustment in the Works Cited section, with the date appearing immediately after the author's name:

Durant, Will, and Ariel Durant. 1965. *The Age of Voltaire.* Vol. 9 of *The Story of Civilization.* New York: Simon & Schuster.

With your parenthetical documentation prepared, you now must turn your attention to the development of a final Works Cited section. You simply have to transcribe those bibliography cards that you actually used to write your paper.

1. Include only works actually cited in the research paper.
2. Arrange all works alphabetically according to author's last name or according to the title of a work if there is no author. Ignore *A, An,* or *The.*
3. Begin each entry at the left margin. Indent by five spaces everything in an entry that comes after the first line.
4. Double-space every line.
5. Punctuate with *periods* after the three main divisions in most entries—author, title, and publishing information.

The sample research paper in this section has a Works Cited page for your evaluation.

Preparing the Final Manuscript   Leave time in your research effort to prepare a neat, clean, attractively designed manuscript. *Research papers must be typed.* Consult your instructor for the desired format, and follow the guidelines for manuscript preparation. Having invested so much time and effort in a research project, you owe it to yourself as well as to the reader to submit a manuscript that has been prepared with extreme care.

A Sample Research Paper

Gurov's Flights of Emotion in Chekhov's "The Lady with the Pet Dog"

Boyd Creasman

In 1921, Conrad Aiken made the following assessment of Anton Chekhov's work: "This, after all, is Chekhov's genius—he was a master of mood" (151).

Indeed Aiken's statement is a good starting point for a discussion of the structure of Chekhov's short fiction. Many of Chekhov's short stories—the later ones in particular—are structured around the main character's moments of strong emotion, a feature of the author's short fiction that has never been fully explored, even in discussions of individual stories. For example, much of the criticism of "The Lady with the Pet Dog," one of Chekhov's most revered short stories, has focused on its parallels with his real life love for Olga Knipper, the influence of Tolstoy's *Anna Karenina*, the story's similarities with Chekhov's later plays, and its exemplification of the author's realism and modernity, which have greatly influenced twentieth-century short fiction. In tracing the story's biographical and literary influences and its relation to other literature, though, Chekhov critics have generally ignored an important feature of "The Lady with the Pet Dog"—namely, the significance of Gurov's two flights of emotion, the first with Anna at Oreanda, the second outside the Medical Club at Moscow.[1] These two moments of intense feeling are crucial to understanding Gurov's motivations and illustrate the importance of this kind of emotional flight to the structure of Chekhov's short fiction.

In the first of his two flights of emotion, Gurov contemplates the transcendence of love as he sits quietly on a bench with Anna at Oreanda:

> Not a leaf stirred, the grasshoppers chirruped, and the monotonous hollow roar of the sea came up to them, speaking of peace, of the eternal sleep lying in wait for us all. The sea had roared like this before there was any Yalta or Oreanda, it was roaring now, and it would go on roaring, just as indifferently and hollowly, when we had passed away. And it may be that in this continuity, this utter indifference to life and death, lies the secret of our ultimate salvation, of the stream of life on our planet, and of its never-ceasing movement toward perfection.
>
> Side by side with a young woman, who looked so exquisite in the early

---

[1] A.P. Chudakov, in *Chekhov's Poetics* (Ann Arbor: Ardis, 1983), comes closest to recognizing the structural importance of such scenes in his discussion of how characters' emotional states affect the presentation of physical detail. See chapter 3, "Narrative from 1895–1904," of Chudakov's book.

light, soothed and enchanted by the sight of all this magical beauty—sea, mountains, clouds and the vast expanse of the sky—Gurov told himself that, when you came to think of it, everything in the world is beautiful really, everything but our own thoughts and actions, when we lost sight of the higher aims of life, and of our dignity as human beings. (226)

This passage reveals one of the strengths of Chekhov's writing, his superb handling of the theme of transcendence through love. In *Anton Chekhov and the Lady with the Pet Dog,* Virginia Llewellyn Smith discusses the importance of this theme: "In Chekhov's later work, this ideal of love was to become increasingly associated with the concept of something above and beyond the transient, or more precisely, with a quasi-philosophical speculative interest, and a quasi-mystical faith in the future of mankind" (138). Another critic, Beverly Hahn, makes a similar point, finding in some of Chekhov's work a "mysterious transcendence . . . of the great moral and philosophical issues of existence" (253). Finding the eternal in a particular moment, Chekhov's characters can turn away mortality and meaninglessness, if only briefly, by turning to each other. However, it is important to remember that at this point in the story, Gurov clearly has not fallen in love with Anna. At first it is not Anna in particular whom he desires, but rather a pretty woman in general, and the reader is told that Gurov, who refers to women as "the lower race," actually "could not have existed a single day" without them (222). Indeed, Gurov enjoys Anna's company at Yalta but is at first surprised, then bored and annoyed with her sense of having sinned. And when Anna must leave Yalta and return to her husband, Gurov does not seem greatly to regret that the affair has apparently ended: "And he told himself that this had been just one more of the many adventures in his life, and that it, too, was over, leaving nothing but a memory . . . " (227). However, when he returns home, he cannot seem to forget the lady with the dog.

   Gurov's second flight of emotion results from his sudden awareness of the grossness and banality of life in Moscow, and the way it pales in comparison to the time he spent with Anna in Yalta. When Gurov starts to tell one of his companions at the Medical Club about her, his friend interrupts him with a comment about dinner, "the sturgeon was just a *leetle* off." At this moment, all of Gurov's pent-up frustrations with his life in Moscow find release in the quintessential Chekhovian flight:

> These words, in themselves so commonplace, for some reason infuriated Gurov, seemed to him humiliating, gross. What savage manners, what people! What wasted evenings, what tedious, empty days! Frantic card-playing, gluttony, drunkenness, perpetual talk always about the same thing. The greater part of one's time and energy went on business that was no use to anyone, and on discussing the same thing over and over again, and there was nothing to show for all of it but a stunted, earth-bound existence and a round of trivialities, and there was nowhere to escape to, you might as well be in a madhouse or a convict settlement. (229)

In some ways, this passage represents the climax of the story, for after Gurov resolves to go to Anna's town, the remainder of the story, in which the characters are forced to keep up appearances by not telling anyone about the affair, has an aura of inevitability about it. In addition to this structural importance, this intense burst of emotion is also very important to an understanding of Gurov's motivations for renewing the affair and thus raises an interesting question: is his decision to find Anna motivated more by love for her or by his desire to escape the tedium of life in Moscow? Certainly the Gurov in the first two sections of the story does not seem like the kind of man who is capable of falling in love with Anna. He becomes bored and uncomfortable, rather than concerned or sensitive, when she gets upset. Does Gurov truly love Anna, or is she simply the natural person for him to turn to in his time of depression?

In his excellent "Chekhov and the Modern Short Story," Charles E. May argues that the question is unanswerable:

> It is never clear in the story whether Gurov truly loves Anna Sergeyevna or whether it is only the romantic fantasy that he wishes to maintain. What makes the story so subtle and complex is that Chekhov presents the romance in such a limited and objective way that we realize that there is no way to determine whether it is love or romance, for there is no way to distinguish between them. (151)

May's otherwise good interpretation is slightly off the mark on this point. While it is true that throughout most of the story it is difficult—because of the objectivity to which May alludes—to determine whether Gurov loves Anna, the reader is directly told just before the conclusion of the story that the two main characters do indeed love each other and that Gurov has "fallen in love properly, thoroughly, for the first time in his life" (234). It is crucial to recognize that the Gurov at the end of the story is not the same as the one at the beginning, and the difference is not merely that he now needs love, but that he has clearly found the woman he loves. Certainly, Gurov does not love less simply because he feels a need for love in his life; in fact, it is precisely this yearning that causes his love for Anna to awaken and grow. And again the key to understanding Gurov's motivations for leaving Moscow and going to Anna is his flights of emotion in which he recognizes the essential truth of the story: his love for Anna is far more noble than his banal, socially acceptable life in Moscow.

Still, at the end of the story, the couple's problem—how to keep their love for each other alive while hiding the relationship from society—remains unresolved. Moreover, neither character seems to have the courage to reveal the truth of their love to anyone else, and therefore, the characters find themselves in a kind of limbo:

> And it seemed to them that they were within an inch of arriving at a decision, and that then a new, beautiful life would begin. And they both realized that the end was still far, far away, and that the hardest, the most complicated part was only just beginning. (235)

Gurov and Anna find themselves in a desperate situation, but as Beverly Hahn suggests, "desperation is not the dominant note of the story, nor is its outcome really tragic, because the hardship of Anna's and Gurov's love cannot be separated from the *fact* of that love and from the fact that it brings each a degree of fulfilment not known before" (253).

With its elegant language, complex main characters, and realistic detail, "The Lady with the Pet Dog" is indeed a masterful story of many moods and, therefore, an illustration of the validity of Conrad Aiken's judgment that Chekhov is a master of mood. Gurov's two intense moments of emotion are important to the structure of the story and demonstrate an important feature of the author's style, for similar Chekhovian flights can be found in many of his other stories, especially his later ones, such as "About Love," "A Visit to Friends," "The Bishop," and "The Betrothed," just to name a few. These flights of emotion are as important in Chekhov's stories as epiphanies are in Joyce's and therefore merit further exploration by those interested in the study of Chekhov's short fiction.

Works Cited

Aiken, Conrad. *Collected Criticism.* London: Oxford UP, 1968.

Chekhov, Anton. "The Lady with the Pet Dog." Trans. Ivy Litvinov. *Anton Chekhov's Short Stories.* Norton Critical Edition. Ed. Ralph E. Matlaw. New York: Norton, 1979. 221–35.

Chudakov, A.P. *Chekhov's Poetics.* Ann Arbor: Ardis, 1983.

Hahn, Beverly. *Chekhov: A Study of the Major Stories and Plays.* Cambridge: Cambridge UP, 1977.

May, Charles E. "Chekhov and the Modern Short Story." *A Chekhov Companion.* Ed. Toby W. Clyman. Westport, CT: Greenwood, 1985. 147–63.

Smith, Virginia Llewellyn. *Anton Chekhov and the Lady with the Pet Dog.* London: Oxford UP, 1973.

Permissions
Acknowledgments

Index